INTEGRATING RESEARCH

ON

TEACHING AND LEARNING

MATHEMATICS

SUNY Series, Reform in Mathematics
Education

Judith Sowder, EDITOR

The preparation of this book was supported by the Office
for Educational Research and Improvement, United States
Department of Education (Grant Number G00870279) and
by the Wisconsin Center for Education Research, School of
Education, University of Wisconsin-Madison. The opinions expressed in this publication do not necessarily reflect
the views of the Office for Educational Research and Improvement or the Wisconsin Center for Education Research.

INTEGRATING RESEARCH

ON

TEACHING AND LEARNING

MATHEMATICS

Edited by
Elizabeth Fennema
Thomas P. Carpenter
Susan J. Lamon

State University of New York Press

Published by
State University of New York Press, Albany

For information, address the State University of New York Press,
State University Plaza, Albany, NY 12246

Production by Christine M. Lynch
Marketing by Bernadette LaManna

Library of Congress Cataloging-in-Publication Data

Integrating research on teaching and learning mathematics / edited by
    Elizabeth Fennema, Thomas P. Carpenter, Susan J. Lamon.
        p. cm. — (SUNY series, reform in mathematics.   Education)
    "The First Wisconsin Symposium for Research on Teaching and
    Learning Mathematics took place in May 1988 in Madison, Wisconsin,
    and sponsored by the Instruction/Learning Works Group"—P. 11.
    Includes bibliographical references.
    ISBN 0-7914-0522-2 (alk. paper). — ISBN 0-7914-0523-0 (pbk. :
    alk. paper)
    1. Mathematics—Study and teaching—Research—Congresses.
    I. Fennema, Elizabeth.   II. Carpenter, Thomas P.   III. Lamon, Susan
    J., 1949 –   .   IV. Wisconsin Symposium on Research on Teaching
    and Learning Mathematics (1st : 1988 : Madison, Wis.).   V. National
    Center for Research in Mathematical Sciences Education.
    Instruction/Learning Work Group.   VI. Series.
    QA11.A1I446   1991
    510′.71—dc20   90-9709
                                                                         CIP

10   9   8   7   6   5   4   3   2   1

CONTENTS

PREFACE

In the last decade, there have been significant advances in the study of students' learning and problem solving in mathematics and in the study of classroom instruction. For the most part, however, these two programs of research have been conducted in relative isolation from one another. There is a growing awareness among researchers that an integrated program of research is needed that takes into account what we know about students' learning and what we know about classroom instruction. This monograph represents the efforts of researchers with diverse backgrounds to address the problem of developing a unified paradigm for studying teaching that builds upon both cognitive and instructional research.

The papers in this monograph approach the problem from different perspectives. Three papers are concerned with how explicit knowledge about students' thinking may be applied to the study of classroom instruction. Carpenter and Fennema as well as Cobb, Yackel, and Wood discuss how knowledge about children's thinking and problem solving may be used to design and study instruction in classrooms. Hiebert and Wearne consider the same basic problem, but they are primarily concerned with the level of knowledge about students' thinking that is necessary to draw implications for instruction. Lampert as well as Post, Harel, Behr, and Lesh build more upon the methods of cognitive research than upon the knowledge gained from that research. They discuss research programs in which paradigms based on cognitive research are applied to the study of classroom instruction and teachers' mathematical knowledge. Starting with the perspective of a researcher involved in the study of teaching, Grouws points out the importance of building on recent research on classroom instruction in mathematics as well as on cognitive research. The paper by McLeod argues that we must consider affective as well as cognitive factors in our research, and Secada cautions that knowledge of diverse groups must be part of the research equation.

This monograph grew out of a conference sponsored by the National Center for Research in Mathematical Sciences Education (NCRMSE), which is supported by the United States Office of Educational Research and Improvement. The mission of the Center is to provide a research base for the reform movement in school mathematics. The Center is organized into two working groups: The Instruction/ Learning Working Group and the Curriculum/Assessment Working Group. The basic problem being addressed by the Instruction/Learning Work Group is how to build relationships between current research on students' cognition and problem solving and research on instruction. The Curriculum/Assessment group is addressing some of the fundamental assumptions and issues raised by the current reform movement, studying current curricular and assessment practices, and investigating the influence of assessment on the curriculum.

The First Wisconsin Symposium for Research on Teaching and Learning Mathematics took place in May 1988 in Madison, Wisconsin, and was sponsored by the Instruction/Learning Work Group. The conference brought together researchers engaged in the study of students' thinking and problem solving and researchers engaged in the study of teaching. The goal of the conference was to initiate a dialogue among researchers with diverse backgrounds who were concerned with the problem of integrating cognitive and instructional research in mathematics education in order to provide direction to research in this area. The papers included in this volume represent only a part of that discussion.

We are indebted to a number of individuals for the success of the conference and the production of this volume. We would like to thank Randolph Philipp and Deborah Carey for their skillful handling of the many administrative details of the conference. We also would like to thank Geri McGinnis for typing the manuscripts and assisting with the conference in a variety of ways. Finally, we thank the entire staff at the Wisconsin Center for Education Research for facilitating not only the conference, but all of the work conducted by the Center.

1

Research and Cognitively Guided Instruction*

Thomas P. Carpenter and Elizabeth Fennema

In their chapter in the third edition of the *Handbook of Research on Teaching*, Romberg and Carpenter (1986) proposed that research on children's thinking and research on teaching represent two distinct disciplines of scientific inquiry, which have resulted in substantial knowledge. However, this knowledge has not been integrated in any meaningful way. In this chapter, we will briefly review what knowledge we have gained from the two distinct lines of inquiry and propose a model for integrating research on teaching and learning.

RESEARCH ON TEACHING

Since the mid-1960s, we have learned a great deal from the research on teaching. We have learned about the way teachers in actual classrooms do such things as interact with children, monitor children's work, respond to children, and provide feedback to children. Researchers have gathered data about the frequency with which teachers engage

*The preparation of this paper was supported in part by a grant from the National Science Foundation (Grant No. MDR-8550236). The opinions expressed in this paper do not necessarily reflect the position, policy, or endorsement of the National Science Foundation.

in various types of behavior (such as praise or questioning) and the relationship of the frequency of these behaviors to children's achievement. (For a thorough discussion of what has been learned, see Brophy & Good, 1986.) Much of the research has been acquired since the mid-1960s within a research paradigm called "process-product." Process-product studies have focused on teachers' and students' behaviors (the processes) that produce gains in students' achievement (the product). From these studies, researchers have identified the behaviors that characterize effective teaching, that is, teaching behaviors that are related to achievement gain. They have defined these behaviors as active teaching or direct instruction (Good, Grouws, & Ebmeier, 1983).

One limitation of process-product studies is that they have focused on what teachers do and should do. Children have been largely ignored in this type of research, and children's thinking and learning during instruction have not been the focus of teacher training. A major limitation of product-process research is that teachers' thought processes before, during, and after instruction have been largely ignored. Shulman and Elstein (1975) suggested that to gain a more complete understanding of how classroom instruction affects students' learning, researchers need to view the teacher not only as one who engages in certain classroom behaviors, but also as an active processor of information before, during, and after classroom instruction.

The rationale for this perspective of the teacher was presented most clearly in a report produced by Panel 6 as part of the National Conference on Studies in Teaching that was convened by the National Institute of Education in June, 1974. The panelists argued that:

> It is obvious that what teachers do is directed in no small measure by what they think. Moreover, it will be necessary for any innovation in the context, practices, and technology of teaching to be mediated through the minds and motives of

teachers. To the extent that observed or intended teacher behavior is "thoughtless," it makes no use of the human teachers' most unique attributes. In so doing, it becomes mechanical and might well be done by a machine. If, however, teaching is done and, in all likelihood, will continue to be done by human teachers, the question of the relationships between thought and action becomes crucial (National Institute of Education, 1975, p. 1).

Research on teachers' thought processes and decisions has burgeoned in the decade since the publication of the Panel 6 report. Comprehensive reviews of this research have been done by Shavelson and Stern (1981) and more recently by Clark and Peterson (1986). Rather than attempt to provide an exhaustive review of this research here, we will briefly summarize Clark and Peterson's conclusions.

First, research shows that thinking plays an important part in teaching. Clark and Peterson (1986) concluded that the image of a teacher as a reflective professional is not farfetched. As thoughtful professionals, teachers have more in common with physicians and lawyers than they have in common with technicians. Second, the research shows that teachers' plans have real consequences in the classroom. Third, during interactive teaching, teachers are continually thinking and they report making decisions frequently — once every two minutes. Fourth, teachers have theories and belief systems that influence their perceptions, plans, and actions in the classroom.

The research on teachers' thought processes further substantiates that the teacher is a reflective, thoughtful individual. Moreover, the research documents that teaching is a complex and cognitively demanding human process. Teachers' beliefs, knowledge, judgments, thoughts, and decisions have a profound effect on the way they teach as well as on students' learning in their classroom. In addition, teachers' beliefs, thoughts, judgments, knowledge, and decisions affect how they perceive and think about pre- and

in-service training and new curricula, and the extent to
which they implement the training and curricula as intended by the developers.

Most research on teacher cognitions has studied elementary school teachers and has taken place without consideration of the content of instruction. As a consequence,
researchers have not directly investigated the problem of
teachers' cognitions during mathematics instruction. Further, they have not addressed questions regarding the
knowledge base that students bring to instruction, how
this knowledge influences or should influence the content
and organization of instruction, and how student knowledge changes as a result of instruction.

RESEARCH ON CHILDREN'S THINKING

One of the central assumptions underlying most current research on children's thinking and problem solving is that
students are not passive learners who simply absorb knowledge. Students bring a great deal of knowledge to almost
any learning situation. Some of the knowledge is correct,
and some is incorrect. Some knowledge facilitates learning, and some hinders it. Nevertheless, learning is influenced by children's pre-instructional knowledge, and to
understand the effects of instruction, teachers and researchers need to first understand the nature of that knowledge and how it influences what children learn.

In a number of areas, research is beginning to provide
a profile of the knowledge that children bring to instruction. For example, there are substantial bodies of research
regarding children's informal knowledge in early number
(Carpenter & Moser, 1983; Fuson, 1988; Riley, Greeno, &
Heller, 1983), rational numbers (Hiebert & Behr, 1988), and
algebra (Wagner & Kieran, 1989). The research also provides a framework for analyzing students' errors and misconceptions. The work of Brown and Burton (1978), Matz
(1980), and others indicate that many errors are not caused
from failing to learn a particular idea, but from learning or
constructing the wrong idea. This research provides a ba-

sis for identifying the misconceptions underlying buggy algorithms which, in turn, can serve as a framework for designing both initial instruction to reduce the factors that lead to errors, and programs for remediating the errors once they have been identified.

The role of understanding in learning mathematics is an issue of increasing importance to current research. Research on meaningful learning dates back over fifty years (see Brownell, 1935) and the proposition that understanding facilitates retention and transfer has repeatedly been documented since Brownell's initial work (Resnick & Ford, 1981). While early studies generally sidestepped the problem of defining understanding, current research is seeking explicit definitions of understanding in relation to particular concepts or skills (Greeno, 1978; Hiebert, 1986). In general, understanding is characterized as interconnected knowledge. This network analogy suggests the critical importance of relating new knowledge that is the object of instruction to the existing knowledge that the learner brings to instruction.

Another instructional issue for which thinking and problem solving research may provide some insights concerns the selection and sequencing of mathematics content. These studies are beginning to provide a picture of skilled performance in a variety of areas and of how the knowledge of experts differs from that of novices (Chi, Glaser, & Rees, 1982). One way of applying this research would be to design instruction to explicitly teach knowledge and procedures that represent expert performance.

In addressing the issue of sequencing content, Case (1983) proposed that since most concepts and skills develop over time and in relatively well-defined sequences, instruction should recapitulate that sequence of development. In other words, children should be explicitly taught the knowledge and procedures of each succeeding stage of development.

Although Case has designed successful instructional programs based on this principle, other sequences are equally plausible. By the same token, it is not apparent that it is productive to teach all children the problem-solving techniques of highly skilled problem solvers. Thus, it is premature to say that research on children's thinking provides clear guidelines for selecting and sequencing instruction. However, this research encourages the investigation of instructional sequences which are different than those in place in most classrooms.

The contribution of the research on children's thinking processes is not limited to rich descriptions of children's cognitions. Of equal importance is its powerful methodology. The techniques developed to study children's thinking and problem solving provide a practical means by which teachers might assess the knowledge of their students, and they offer other researchers more sensitive measures of the effects of instruction.

Researchers on children's thinking and problem solving have been particularly concerned with performance within specific mathematical content areas. In the process of analyzing children's thinking and problem solving, they have provided detailed analyses of the structure of knowledge and procedures within different content domains, what constitutes successful performance within the domains, specific misconceptions and buggy procedures, and the stages that children pass through in acquiring expertise (Carpenter, Moser, & Romberg, 1982; Ginsburg, 1983; Hiebert, 1986; Lesh & Landau, 1983). However, for the most part, these researchers have provided a static picture of children's problem solving at particular points in time; they have not yet successfully addressed the question of how children acquire more advanced strategies or how their strategies are influenced by instruction.

SUMMARY

Researchers studying teaching have focused on instruction and teachers' cognitions during instruction, but generally have not been concerned with the content that is taught. In contrast, researchers on children's cognitions have been concerned with what is learned, but for the most part they have not addressed the question of how learning is facilitated. Another difference between the two programs of research is the focus of investigation. Researchers on children's thinking have focused on performance of individual children, whereas researchers on teaching have studied groups of children in regular classroom settings. Thus researchers on teaching have more directly investigated the problems of classroom instruction and how to improve it. On the other hand, researchers on children's cognitions have been more concerned with understanding children's understanding and have provided a much richer analysis of individual performance than is found in most studies of teaching. Moreover, they would argue that the group measures used by process-product researchers, in particular, standardized achievement tests, provide incomplete pictures of performance.

What is needed is a research paradigm that blends the concern for the realities of classroom instruction and teachers' cognitions that are found in research on teaching with the concern for individual students' cognitions and the rich analysis of the structure of mathematics that is found in research on thinking and problem solving. Such a program would have as a goal the identification of principles of instruction that are consistent with: (1) what is known about students' learning, thinking, and problem solving; and (2) what is known about teachers as active, thoughtful professionals. This program should draw on the knowledge that has been gained both from cognitive science and instructional science research.

A MODEL FOR INTEGRATING COGNITIVE AND INSTRUCTIONAL SCIENCE

A general model for research and curriculum development is presented in Figure 1-1. Initial studies suggest that the model provides a promising new paradigm for the study of teaching and learning (Carpenter et al., 1988; Fennema, Carpenter, & Peterson, 1989; Peterson, Fennema, & Carpenter, 1989). This model integrates the perspectives of

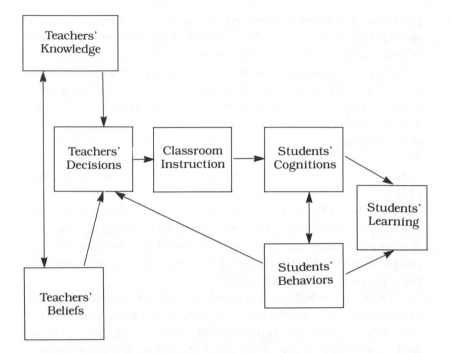

Figure 1-1. Model for research and curriculum development.

cognitive and instructional science to study teachers' pedagogical content knowledge (Shulman, 1986), teachers' beliefs, and how teachers' knowledge and beliefs influence
classroom instruction and students' learning.

This model assigns a central role to teachers' and students' thinking. Classroom instruction is based on teachers' decisions, and the effects of instruction on students'
behaviors and learning are mediated by students' cognitions. As indicated in Figure 1-1, teachers' decisions are
presumed to be based on their knowledge and beliefs as well
as their assessment of students' knowledge through their
observation of students' behaviors.

In a number of areas (for example, early number, rational number, algebra, geometry) there is a structured,
reasonably coherent body of pedagogical knowledge regarding the development of students' concepts and skills.

Within certain domains, there exist detailed analyses of both problem types and student problem-solving processes. These content and strategy analyses provide useful frameworks for relating the components in Figure 1-1. Teachers' pedagogical knowledge and beliefs, classroom instruction, and students' cognitions and learning all can be studied in terms of the content framework. In each domain, the framework provides a basis to study teachers' knowledge of different problems, their knowledge of the relative difficulty of those problems, and their knowledge of the different strategies that children use to solve the problems.

The characterization of students' problem-solving processes provides a framework to evaluate learning and problem solving both for research purposes and to aid teachers' instructional decision making. The analysis of both the problems and the development of students' problem-solving abilities makes it possible to select critical problems that differentiate between levels of performance. The techniques developed to investigate students' problem-solving processes also make it possible to assess students' knowledge and understanding at a deeper level than can be determined by mere correct or incorrect responses. As a consequence, it is possible to characterize students' performance in terms of acquired concepts or skills rather than simply in terms of scores on a test. The content and strategy frameworks are also useful in developing measures of transfer and problem solving that are clearly related to the knowledge and skills being taught and relatively sensitive to the effects of instruction.

The ability to characterize the knowledge and/or performance makes it possible to examine specific relationships between the different components of Figure 1-1 with a much higher degree of specificity than has been possible in previous studies. For example, it is possible to establish links between teachers' knowledge and how that knowledge is translated into specific classroom activities, or to investigate how particular instructional activities are reflected in students' learning of the concepts and skills being taught.

One of the key relationships in the model in Figure 1-1 is the relationship between teachers' decisions and teachers' assessment of students' thinking. In the figure, this relationship is represented by the arrows joining students' cognitions, students' behaviors, and teachers' decisions. A basic assumption of the model is that one of the principal ways that teachers apply pedagogical knowledge is in the assessment of their own students' knowledge and abilities.

COGNITIVELY GUIDED INSTRUCTION

Conceiving teaching in terms of teachers' knowledge and decision making is important for understanding teachers' planning and classroom instruction. In addition, it provides a perspective for analyzing the impact of teacher training programs and the implementation of new curricula as well as a basis for designing programs of instruction and teacher education. Teachers' beliefs and knowledge not only have a profound effect on the decisions they make regarding instruction, but they also influence how teachers respond to teacher education programs and new programs of instruction.

A major focus of our research has been to study the effects of programs designed to teach teachers about learners' thinking and problem solving and how to use that information to design and implement instruction (Fennema, Carpenter, & Peterson, 1989; Carpenter et al., 1988; Peterson, Fennema, Carpenter, & Loef, 1989). Instruction for teachers in our experimental treatment has focused on teachers' pedagogical knowledge. Rather than attempting to prescribe a program of instruction or even a series of procedures for instruction, we have been studying how to help teachers use knowledge from cognitive science to make their own instructional decisions. This approach, which we call *Cognitively Guided Instruction*, is based on the premise that the teaching-learning process is too complex to specify in advance, and as a consequence, teaching essentially is problem solving. Instruction must necessarily be mediated by teachers' decisions, and we can ultimately bring about the most significant changes in instruction by helping teachers to make more informed decisions rather than by attempting to program them to perform in a particular way.

The guiding principle for Cognitively Guided Instruction is that instructional decisions should be based on careful analyses of students' knowledge and the goals of instruction. Thus, teachers must have a thorough knowledge of the content domain, and they must be able to effectively assess their students' knowledge in this domain. Knowledge of the content integrates content and pedagogical knowledge. It includes an understanding of distinctions between problems that are reflected in students' solutions at different stages in acquiring expertise in the domain. Teachers must have knowledge of problem difficulty as well as knowledge of distinctions between problems that result in different processes of solution. The ability to assess their own students' knowledge also requires that teachers have an understanding of the general stages that students pass through in acquiring the concepts and procedures in the domain, the processes that are used to solve different problems at each stage, and the nature of the knowledge that underlies these processes.

Although instructional practices have not been prescribed, there are broad principles of instruction that underlie our approach. The basic principle that is embedded in all the other principles, is that insofar as possible, instruction should be appropriate for each student. This means that problems, concepts, or procedures being learned should have meaning for each student. For a task to have meaning, the student should be able to relate it to the knowledge that he or she already possesses. Instructional decisions should be based on regular assessment of each student's knowledge throughout the course of instruction. Other broad principles are that instruction should be organized to involve students to actively construct their own knowledge with understanding, and that instruction should stress relationships among concepts, skills, and problem solving.

Principles of assessment have also been identified. One key perspective on assessment is that it is important to know not only whether a learner can solve a particular problem, but also how the learner solves the problem. By watching learners solve problems and listening to them explain how they solved them, researchers examining mathematics learning and problem solving have effectively identified the mental processes used to solve problems. The techniques used in this research provide a model for classroom assessment.

Research Questions

The underlying question that guides the research of the Instruction/Learning Working Group of the National Center is: How can knowledge from cognitive and instructional science be integrated to design more effective instruction in mathematics? Several major questions are embedded in this basic question:

- How can research on students' cognition be applied to problems of classroom instruction?
- What kinds of knowledge about students' thinking and problem solving are most useful for addressing problems of instruction? What additional knowledge is needed?
- Can we develop paradigms for studying classroom instruction that are consistent with what we know about individual student's learning and problem solving?

We propose that the paradigm for integrating cognitive and instructional science proposed by Fennema, Carpenter, and Peterson (1989) as discussed above is one approach for addressing these questions. From this approach comes a number of more specific questions related to the major questions listed above.

- What general knowledge and beliefs about students' thinking and problem solving do teachers hold? How are teachers' knowledge and beliefs related to the decisions they make about instruction? How are these decisions related to student outcomes?

- What do teachers know about their own students' thinking and problem solving? How does this knowledge influence their instruction? How are their decisions about instruction based on this knowledge related to student outcomes?
- How do teachers' beliefs relate to their instructional practices? Do teachers' beliefs about males and females of different ethnic/racial backgrounds influence their instructional interactions with children?
- Can teachers use information from research on students' thinking and problem solving to more effectively assess their students and make more informed instructional decisions? How are these decisions related to student outcomes?
- How is information from cognitive and instructional science research best transmitted to teachers? How does providing teachers with this knowledge influence the teachers' instruction and subsequently their students' learning?
- What kinds of knowledge about students and about instructional practice have the greatest influence on teachers' decisions and actions? What additional knowledge about students and about teaching is most critically needed to allow teachers to more effectively assess their students' learning and make more informed instructional decisions?

In conclusion, it is safe to say that there is considerable knowledge about how children learn mathematics and about how teachers function as instructional decision makers. Research programs are needed to integrate these two sets of knowledge. In a number of domains, enough is known so that research programs should be able to develop curricula that help learners gain mathematical knowledge with understanding. While the integrating research model presented here is not the only model which will result in significant new knowledge, all components of the Cognitively Guided Instruction (CGI) model and their interrelationships must be considered as research programs are designed. When the relationships between such components are considered, research will provide information that will enable teachers to teach in such a way that most students learn mathematics with understanding.

REFERENCES

Brophy, J., & Good, T. L. (1986). Teacher behavior and student achievement. In M. C. Wittrock (Ed.), *Handbook of research on teaching* (3rd ed., pp. 328–375). New York: Macmillan.

Brown, J. S., & Burton, R. R. (1978). Diagnostic models for procedural bugs in basic mathematical skills. *Cognitive Science, 2,* 153–192.

Brownell, W. A. (1935). Psychological considerations in the learning and the teaching of arithmetic. In W. D. Reeve (Ed.), *The teaching of arithmetic: The tenth yearbook of the National Council of Teachers of Mathematics* (pp. 1–31). New York: Teachers College Press.

Carpenter, T. P., Fennema, E., Peterson, P. L., & Carey, D. A. (1988). Teachers' pedagogical content knowledge of students' problem solving in elementary arithmetic. *Journal for Research in Mathematics Education, 19*(5), 385–401.

Carpenter, T. P., Moser, J. M., & Romberg, T. A. (1982). *Addition and subtraction: A cognitive perspective.* Hillsdale, NJ: Lawrence Erlbaum Associates.

Case, R. (1983). *Intellectual development: A systematic reinterpretation.* New York: Academic Press.

Chi, M. T. H., Glaser, R., & Rees, E. (1982). Expertise in problem solving. In R. Sternberg (Ed.), *Advances in the psychology of human intelligence* (pp. 7–75). Hillsdale, NJ: Lawrence Erlbaum Associates.

Clark, C. M., & Peterson, P. L. (1986). Teachers' thought processes. In M. C. Wittrock (Ed.), *Handbook of research on teaching* (3rd ed., pp. 255–296). New York: Macmillan.

Fennema, E., Carpenter, T. P., & Peterson, P. L. (1989). Teachers' decision making and cognitively guided instruction: A new paradigm for curriculum development. In N. F. Ellerton & M. A.

(Ken) Clements (Eds.), *School mathematics: The challenge to change* (pp. 174 – 187). Geelong, Victoria, Australia: Deakin University Press.

Fennema, E., Carpenter, T. P., & Peterson, P. L. (in press). Learning Mathematics with Understanding. In J. Brophy (Ed.), *Advances in research on teaching* (Vol. 1). Greenwich, CT: JAI Press.

Fuson, K. C. (1988). *Children's counting and concepts of number.* New York: Springer-Verlag.

Ginsburg, H. P. (Ed.). (1983). *The development of mathematical thinking.* New York: Academic Press.

Good, T. L., Grouws, D. A., & Ebmeier, H. (1983). *Active mathematics teaching.* New York: Longman.

Greeno, J. G. (1978). A study of problem solving. In R. Glaser (Ed.), *Advances in instructional psychology* (Vol. 1, pp. 13 – 75). Hillsdale, NJ: Lawrence Erlbaum Associates.

Hiebert, J. (Ed.). (1986). *Conceptual and procedural knowledge: The case of mathematics.* Hillsdale, NJ: Lawrence Erlbaum Associates.

Hiebert, J., & Behr, M. (1988). *Research agenda for mathematics education: Number concepts and operations in the middle grades.* Reston, VA: National Council of Teachers of Mathematics.

Lesh, R., & Landau, M. (Eds.). (1983). *Acquisition of mathematical concepts and processes.* New York: Academic Press.

Matz, M. (1980). Towards a computation theory of algebraic competence. *The Journal of Mathematical Behavior, 3,* 93 – 166.

National Institute of Education. (1975). *Teaching as clinical information processing: Report of Panel 6, National Conference on Studies in Teaching.* Washington, DC: National Institute of Education.

Peterson, P. L., Fennema, E., Carpenter, T. P., & Loef, M. (1989). Teachers' Pedagogical content beliefs in mathematics. *Cognition and Instruction, 6*(1), 1 – 40.

Resnick, L. B., & Ford, W. W. (1981). *The psychology of mathematics for instruction.* Hillsdale, NJ: Lawrence Erlbaum Associates.

Riley, M. S., Greeno, J. G., & Heller, J. I. (1983). Development of children's problem-solving ability in arithmetic. In H. P. Ginsburg (Ed.), *The development of mathematical thinking* (pp. 153 – 196). New York: Academic Press.

Romberg, T. A., & Carpenter, T. P. (1986). Research on teaching and learning mathematics: Two disciplines of scientific inquiry. In M. C. Wittrock (Ed.), *Handbook of research on teaching* (3rd ed., pp. 850–873). New York: Macmillan.

Shavelson, R. J., & Stern, P. (1981). Research on teachers' pedagogical thoughts, judgments, decisions, and behavior. *Review of Educational Research, 51,* 455–498.

Shulman, L. S. (1986). Paradigms and research programs in the study of teaching: A contemporary perspective. In M. C. Wittrock (Ed.), *Handbook of research on teaching* (3rd ed., pp. 3–36). New York: Macmillan.

Shulman, L. S., & Elstein, A. S. (1975). Studies of problem solving, judgment, and decision making: Implications for educational research. In F. N. Kerlinger (Ed.), *Review of research in education* (Vol. 3, pp. 3–42). Itasca, IL: F. E. Peacock.

Wagner, S., & Kieran, C. (1989). *Research agenda for mathematics education: Research issues in the learning and teaching of algebra.* Reston, VA: National Council of Teachers of Mathematics.

2

Diversity, Equity, and Cognitivist Research*

Walter G. Secada

This paper is about equity in mathematics education research. The specific inquiry concerns the teaching and learning of mathematics in terms of the social arrangements that research legitimates or questions. If disparities in mathematics education among various populations represent unjust social arrangements — the position taken by writers who are concerned with equity in education (Secada, 1989) — then research on the teaching and learning of mathematics should help us to restructure those arrangements. Alternatively, if it merely legitimates the factors and circumstances that gave rise to those disparities, then that research itself must be questioned.

DISPARITIES AND EQUITY

One of the most pressing issues facing us as we move into the next century is that disparities based on socioeconomic

---

*This paper was funded in part by a grant to The Upper Great Lakes Multifunctional Resource Center at the Wisconsin Center for Education Research, through U.S. Department of Education Contract No. 300860050. Opinions, results, conclusions, and recommendations are those of the author and do not have the endorsement of the Department of Education.

Thanks to Lily Wong Fillmore for comments on an earlier draft of this paper.
17

status (class), gender, race, ethnicity, and/or language
background can be found along a broad array of mathematics education indicators. These include careers and post-
secondary degrees in mathematics and related fields,
school achievement in mathematics at virtually all levels,
high school mathematics course taking, and affect related
to mathematics (Oakes, 1987, in press; Secada, 1990).

Concern about these disparities has been expressed in
various forms. Some writers have observed that our society
is becoming increasingly nonwhite, and that by the turn of
the century between 30 and 40 percent of the school age
population will be minority. They argue that our society
cannot afford to allow disparities to continue (Cole & Griffin, 1987; Padilla, 1988). Others argue that disparities represent an unjust distribution of the opportunities for students to learn mathematics within our educational system.
The latter view, or some variant of it, is at the core of work
falling under the rubric of equity in education.

Elsewhere, I (Secada, 1989a, 1989b) have argued that
equity is a qualitative construct that represents an argument concerning the justice of a particular social arrangement. By the term social arrangement, I refer to the complex
web of agreements (explicit and tacit), actions, and outcomes in which we engage as members of our specific culture and society.

Within Western traditions of law, an issue of equity is
one involving justice that goes beyond how a law or an
agreement is written. Equity is an appeal to the spirit, as
opposed to the letter, of the law. This relationship between
equity and justice seems to have been stated first by Aristotle, to whom both McDowell (1981) and Re (1982) trace
Roman, British, and American notions of equity jurispru-
dence:

> There are two kinds of right and wrong conduct
> towards others, one provided for by written ordi-
> nances, the other by unwritten . . . The other kind
> [the unwritten kind] has itself two varieties . . . [of
> which the second variety] makes up for defects in

a community's written code of law. This is what
we call equity; people regard it as just; it is, in
fact, the sort of justice which goes beyond the
written law. (Aristotle, *Rhetoric*, 1981, pp. 63–64)

The essence of equity lies in our ability to acknowledge
that even if our actions are in accord with a particular set
of rules or even if certain social arrangements are established and traditional, the results of those actions or of the
arrangements may still be unjust. Equity goes beyond following rules, even when we have agreed that actions in accord with those rules are meant to achieve a just and desirable outcome. Equity gauges the results of actions or of
social arrangements directly against standards of justice.

Equity-based inquiry in mathematics education could
take a variety of forms. For example, there is a large body of
work that investigates how the disparities in mathematics
education came to be, and that seeks to reduce, if not eliminate, them. This paper does not fall into that category of
equity work. Rather, it is my intent to apply the notion of
equity in a somewhat different manner.

My purpose is to scrutinize cognitivist research on
teaching and learning of mathematics to determine what
social arrangements among groups based on gender, class,
race, ethnicity, and/or language are legitimated and to
question whether the legitimation of such arrangements is
just. Hence, the issue is dual. What social arrangements
are represented and find legitimation in that research? Are
those arrangements just?

COGNITIVIST RESEARCH AND THE LEGITIMATION OF SOCIAL ARRANGEMENTS

What sorts of social arrangements might find legitimation
within cognitivist research in general, and research on the
teaching and learning of mathematics in particular? At
least two characteristics of that research would seem likely
to produce such results as a by-product, if not directly.
First are the tacit agreements that researchers make

among themselves and that allow them to work within their traditions. Second is how cultural norms from the society are transformed within research and thereby find legitimation.

Tacit Agreements Among Researchers

Cognitivist research tries to scrutinize how people think without concern for "complicating factors like affect and cultural issues in an attempt to simplify the research tasks" (McLeod, 1988, p. 6). The tacit claim in such exclusion is that human thought, in its purest forms, can be characterized in ways that are universally applicable regardless of the social contexts in which that thought is applied. Once a characterization of thought within a specific task domain has been completed, all that remains is a cleanup operation of details, that is, culture and affect.

In arguing for an expansion of research in mathematics education, McLeod notes the central role played by affect in the teaching and learning of mathematics. Yet, he allows that the exclusion of affect from this research may have been "reasonable" insofar as "cognitive science is only concerned about *basic* research" (p. 6, emphasis added). I agree with McLeod's observations about the need to expand what counts as cognitivist research. I am willing to concede that the initial exclusion of factors that seem to complicate the research enterprise is a reasonable strategy, but only to start. However, I am unwilling to grant either these initial efforts or their resultant findings the privileged status of being basic. There are other ways of starting the enterprise. The initial restrictions placed upon what counts as research represent a tacit agreement among its practitioners. There is nothing privileged about it, except that traditionally things have been done this way (see Popkewitz, 1984).

Another example of tacit agreements among researchers, even those working in areas with strong theoretical bases, is that cognitivist theories and models of cognition are developed by interpreting what individuals say and/or do. What large numbers of individuals say and do attains privileged status as being normative, and cognitions that are tied to those self-reports and behaviors will achieve the status of being "how people think." What varies from the norm becomes deviant and must be explained in terms of that norm.

Initial observations achieve a privileged status of their own. The first observations set the terms of discourse within which we seek the norm. What comes subsequently is explained in terms of what came first.

Hence, diverse learners are placed in double jeopardy of being considered deviant and marginal. Since culturally diverse populations are excluded from initial research efforts (in the name of simplifying the job of conducting research) and since, almost by definition, their behaviors vary from the norm, their thinking gets treated either as marginal when results are consistent with prior work, or as deviant when results vary from the norm.

In either case, the diminished status of cultural minorities is legitimated due to how research gets done. There is nothing inevitable about such events. Rather, they flow from the tacit agreements among researchers about the way we do our work.

The Transformation of Cultural Norms

The second kind of process by which cognitivist research might legitimate social arrangements that are oppressive to groups from diverse backgrounds is through the cultural norms it emphasizes. As with any domain of inquiry, cognitivist research is a human artifact. It is situated in a specific time and place, and within a given culture that gives that inquiry its meanings (Popkewitz, 1984, 1986). How this inquiry is situated within a culture reflects what is valued — even in the breach as when, for example, it may oppose tacitly accepted ways of viewing and doing things. Though inquiry may be silent about the cultural norms by which it is grounded in a society, either it accepts and supports those norms, or it questions and opposes them.

For example, Kallos and Lundgren (1975) and Sampson (1977, 1981) have argued that, in spite of seeming neutral-

ity, educational psychology, personality and social psychology, and cognitive psychology (respectively) contain elements that are predicated on acceptance of particular
Western norms. These cultural norms include excessive attention to the individual; within the individual, learning
occurs, social deviance gets defined, and cognition takes
place. Sampson (1981) argues that the primacy that cognitive psychology places on the individual as the object of
inquiry leads to "the denial of reality" (p. 735):

> It is my contention that the cognitivist perspec-
> tive offers a portrait of people who are free to en-
> gage in internal mental activity—to plan, decide,
> wish, think, organize, reconcile, and transform
> conflicts within their heads—and yet who remain
> relatively impotent or apparently unconcerned (in
> psychology's world view) about producing actual
> change in their objective social world. In substi-
> tuting thought for action, mental world transfor-
> mations for real world transformations, cognitiv-
> ism veils the objective sources and bases of social
> life and relegates individual potency to the inner
> world of mental gymnastics. (p. 735)

The stress on the individual and mental worlds, as opposed to the objective and social worlds, is a cultural norm
that finds legitimation in various psychologies. Theoretical
statements are made about a person's behaviors and self-reports that are intended to represent something about his or
her inner world. As the external and social worlds get transformed into the inner and personal worlds, external and social issues are transformed into internal and personal
states.

For example, that students from specific backgrounds
tend not to achieve becomes evidence that the students in
question are having problems in learning. Failure to
achieve is objective and social; learning is internal and individual. (We seek to understand the nature of the learning
problems those students are construed as having.) More-

over, though failure to achieve can be viewed in terms of cultural conflict or of other social factors (see Deyhle, 1987; Ogbu, 1978; Ogbu & Matute-Bianchi, 1986), the psychological problem becomes located within the individual, not within the social context in which that individual is found.

Summary

The tacit agreements about what counts as cognitivist research and about the rules for evidence within that research, on the one hand, and the transformation of cultural norms within those rules and agreements, on the other, are two characteristics of cognitivist research that may serve to grant legitimacy to the existing disparities among diverse groups. These groups, and their membership, come to be seen as marginal, deviant, or somehow personally responsible for their status. These results are neither inevitable nor basic. They are social arrangements that find legitimacy through the omission of the groups and through the transformation of the majority's cultural norms within cognitivist research.

In the following sections, I will explore these themes within the research on the learning and teaching of mathematics. I will present three case studies from that research: the learning of addition and subtraction, teachers' cognitions, and student thinking during classroom instruction. Though issues of student diversity may have been excluded as a means of simplifying the research problem, I will present perspectives and work that are in opposition to current efforts. The need to develop lines of work that bridge these oppositions are one reason for addressing issues of diversity from the start. A second reason is that to wait for subsequent work to address issues of student diversity is to situate the later work within theoretical contexts and discourse that have been set by previous efforts. Hence, the impact of such efforts will be diminished and marginal if the results are consistent with, but not part of, the core; or it will be oppositional and deviant, if results are inconsistent with what is normative.

RESEARCH ON ADDITION AND SUBTRACTION

Research on children's initial solutions of addition and
subtraction p.oblems is one domain that has taken a
strongly cognitive turn. Research has moved from investigations of number fact difficulty, the time taken to memo-
rize those facts, and the role of problem structures on problem difficulty to investigating how word problems are
represented in the mind, the strategies that children actually use to solve problems, and the relationship of problem semantic structure to the development of understandings and solution strategies. (See Carpenter & Moser,
1983; Resnick & Ford, 1981; Romberg & Carpenter, 1986,
for reviews.) This work paints a coherent picture of development. Children understand problems through the use of
increasingly powerful mental representations and structures or schemes. From these representational schemes are
generated children's problem-solving strategies.

     Initially, for a small set of word problems, children's
problem-solving strategies consist of the direct modeling of
the problem's action sequences using objects. These initial
strategies cannot be applied readily across different kinds
of word problems. Hence, at first, there are strong links
among the problems' semantic structures, children's representational schemes, and their problem-solving strategies.

     Over time, children develop increasingly powerful rep-
resentational schemes and problem solving strategies. The
links that tie problem meaning, the child's understanding
of that meaning, and the strategy that is generated from
that understanding become loosened. De Corte and Verschaffel (1987) argue that the links are not loosened as
much as suggested by prior research. These two developments enable children to apply a greater range of modeling
strategies across an increasingly broad range of problems.

     Some problems, such as those in which the first quan-
tity is indeterminate or those in which the action sequence
is ambiguous, remain difficult for children to solve through
direct modeling. In these cases, children must transform

the problem's representation and apply a strategy other than one that matches the problem's semantic structures.

Hence, initial problem difficulty is a function of three things. The first includes the semantic and, to a lesser degree, syntactic structures of the problems, which would seem to require that children possess representational schemes that are powerful enough for them to understand the problem. The second is that the child possess problem-solving strategies that can be linked to the representational schemes. Thirdly, strategies must be executed correctly (see Kintsch & Greeno, 1985; Nesher, 1982).

All of the modeling strategies depend on the child's eventually counting a set of objects. Over time, children's counting skills become increasingly sophisticated. They learn to count sets while simultaneously creating the representation for the set that is being counted; also, they learn to count up and down from arbitrary numbers (Fuson, 1988). These skills get applied as strategies across problem types. The availability of these more powerful strategies allows children to solve problems that they could not solve before and to solve problems that they can already model more easily and effectively. Though there is some question about how strongly the counting strategies are tied to the semantic structures of word problems (De Corte & Verschaffel, 1987), they do resemble children's initial modeling strategies.

Concurrently, children have been memorizing certain number facts, primarily those linked to doubles. Over time these facts get linked to children's other strategies as derived fact strategies (see Carpenter & Moser, 1983, for descriptions). Children, by second or third grade—and even some adults—rely on a mixture of memorized facts, derived facts, counting strategies, and pocket calculators for solving a broad range of addition and subtraction problems.

Two Low Achieving, Omitted Groups

Consider this developmental pattern and two populations whose achievement differs from majority populations as early as first grade: hearing impaired children (Moores,

1976, 1978; Myklebust, 1964) and children of limited English proficiency (LEP). Because the students in question either cannot hear or cannot speak English, their learning of mathematics is seen as related to these deficiencies (for example, see Broadbent & Daniele, 1982; Mestre, 1988). Hence, the research agenda for these groups is usually one of identifying deficiencies in problem solving and oral English as compared to the norms established by research involving the majority population. However, by characterizing children solely in terms of their deficiencies and correlating those deficiencies to each other, we often lose sight of their competencies. This idea is not original; Gelman (1978) made the same point when discussing general research on child development over a decade ago.

American Sign Language. Many hearing impaired children use American Sign Language (or some variant) for communication. These children produce the number word string via their fingers. In contrast, the counting strategies described by Carpenter and Moser (1983), and by others, involve the oral production of the number words together with a visual/kinaesthetic production of units that represent the set being counted.

   In a study involving hearing impaired users of sign language, I (Secada, 1982) gave a group of third- and fourth-grade children a series of part-part-whole subtraction tasks in which the size of the unknown part (the difference) was manipulated: small versus large. Children's strategies were qualitatively different from those that have been reported in the literature for majority populations. They created cardinal representations for one of the parts on one of their hands and counted on using the other part's cardinality as the starting point. Since one of the parts was not known, each child had to create an estimate for the unknown part. What varied, as a function of size, was how that estimate was created and used.

   If the unknown part was small, the child would keep a cardinal representation of his or her estimate on the fingers of one hand. The child would count-on starting from the known part, using the other hand for producing the number-sign string. Counting would continue until the sum was reached. If the total on the counting hand matched the original whole, then the cardinal representation on the noncounting hand was the correct answer. Since a record of the unknown part's estimated size was always available, children could modify the estimates, and they would get the answer, on average, in less than two trials.

When the unknown set (difference) was large, however, a child would have to create the known set's cardinal representation on one hand. The unknown cardinality would be represented on the hand used for counting-on. As the child counted-on to find the sum, he or she would also lose the record for the unknown part's estimate. Hence, after the resultant sum had been checked, the child would have often forgotten what number he or she had started with. Under this condition, children would often make a correct guess for the unknown part, but having lost the record of their estimate, they would need additional trials — sometimes as many as twelve — before finally getting the answer. Estimates, which initially might cluster around the answer, would begin to vary almost wildly, and sometimes, the child would give up before actually producing the answer.

Bilingualism. It is not at all unfair to characterize the bulk of the research involving the mathematical cognitions of Hispanic LEP students as relating low mathematics achievement to low English skills. De Avila and Duncan (1981) found a strong relationship between degree of English proficiency and mathematics achievement along various measures of each. Mestre (1988) presents a detailed analysis of how Hispanic college students missolve the students and professor problem. He argues that their error patterns are qualitatively different from those of monolingual English-speaking students, and hence that those errors are due to the students' Spanish-speaking backgrounds. Cuevas (1984) has developed a teacher training effort based on mathematical English that bilingual children are hypothesized to be missing. Crandall and her associates (Crandall, et al., 1987, in press; Spanos, et al., 1988) have been engaged in validating an extensive curriculum based on teaching bilingual students to analyze the linguistic features of mathematical word problems. The view that language-based deficiencies cause problems in the learning of mathematics has been extended to the case of students who speak Black English (Orr, 1987; Secada, 1988).

Yet for LEP students, an alternative conception is also available. Again, rather than consider them in terms of their deficiencies, we might consider their competence in two languages: English and their native language. In this sense, they are children who are becoming bilingual. Bilingual speakers can enter into a situation and produce the same output, but in either of two languages. There is ample research evidence that children as young as five switch back and forth between their languages, oftentimes using terms borrowed from the other language, rapidly and in response to contextual cues that it is appropriate to do so (Zentella, 1981, 1987). Bilingual speakers have at their disposal two (or more) language production systems that can be used in highly similar contexts.

Early on, bilingual children develop the ability to distinguish between their languages in terms of each language's semantic and syntactic structures (Ianco-Worrall, 1972; Ben-Zeev, 1977). This literature suggests that bilingual children, as a function of degree of bilingualism, become free from some of the semantic constraints of language. For example, Ben-Zeev gave bilingual children a word substitution task in which they had to substitute one part of speech for another within a sentence. That substitution would violate the word's conventional use in normal speech. For example, instead of saying *into* (a preposition), a child was supposed to say *clean* (an adjective or a verb). The correct sentence for this trial would be, "The doll is going clean [into] the house." Bilingual children, who scored below their monolingual peers on the WISC-R, outperformed their peers on tasks like this. Diaz (1983) and McLaughlin (1986) present more detailed discussions concerning the cognitive benefits to being bilingual.

More specific to mathematics, Duran (1988) has found that, for adult Hispanic bilinguals, competence in Spanish correlates with logical reasoning even after controlling for SES and English language proficiency; that is, there is a relationship between degree of bilingualism and logical reasoning. Saxe (1988) proposes that this ability to work with language in an arbitrary manner might have counterparts in the case of mathematical language, the arbitrariness of the counting words being an example. In my own work (Secada, in press), I am pursuing the question of whether or not bilingual children demonstrate their enhanced linguistic abilities in solving arithmetic word problems. Specifically, I am investigating the relationship between degree of bilingualism and problem-solving performance as well as strategy usage. Of particular interest is the question of whether or not bilingual children apply modeling strategies in ways that are different from those reported by previous research.

What Is the Correct World View?

Research indicates that the arithmetic learning of these two excluded populations involves more capacity and certainly more complexity than can be grasped by merely trying to understand deficiencies. The issue that arises is how that capacity should be incorporated into the existing descriptions of development.

Assume for a moment that the norm is to be bilingual— as it is in much of the world. Then, from the beginning, we would have pursued a line of research based on the premise of the cognitive advantages of being bilingual. The picture of the normal development for addition and subtraction would be one in which a small set of modeling strategies developed within a few contexts. Over time, these strategies would become semantically free, and they would be applied across an increasingly broad domain of word problems.

In such a world, we would be worrying about the deviant behavior of monolingual children who would seem unable to free themselves from the semantic constraints of the word problems they were encountering. We would be looking for models of comprehension and learning by which their deficient performance would be explained. In such a world, we would probably try to understand these children's deficiencies: The lack of dual language competence and limited flexibility in applying strategies to new problems. (A similar picture could be drawn for a world that used sign language.)

And this is precisely the point. The current picture for development of addition and subtraction is coherent, but incomplete. The research by which it was developed has attended to—as it should—the majority case. But, by excluding minority children from its concerns, it legitimates an ongoing view of them as deviant. Campbell (1989) discusses how bias has crept into educational research in general by the practice of excluding groups defined as deviant, but then generalizing results to apply to those groups.

The issue is more than just one of individual differences versus universals. These particular differences are related to membership in specific groups in our society. To cast them as individual differences is to marginalize them, since the numbers represented by the individuals who display them cannot (currently) compete with the majority in terms of being judged normal.

Do we then develop many separate descriptions for the development of addition and subtraction; or do we append results such as these to the extant description as caveats? An option quite close to the former is the one taken by proponents of the new scholarship on women (for example, *Educational Researcher,* 1986). They argue that women's particular ways of knowing the world have been lost by research and historical traditions that have been dominated by an overly narrow view of valid knowledge. Their effort represents an attempt to reclaim what has been lost.

The option of integrating results into the coherent corpus might seem preferable on aesthetic and practical grounds. After all, a few studies do not a theory make. Yet the manner in which children's unique ways of thinking about arithmetic will enter that corpus remains an issue. These children could still remain deviant and marginalized: "This is how things normally develop. Oh yes, the asterisks refer to some special cases." Or, their ways of solving problems could be reported in ways that give it as much legitimacy as the normal (that is, larger) populations. What makes the latter option problematic is that the model has already been set. The terms of discourse and the ways in which we speak about the phenomena are so determined that what is "other" seems to be deviant. Consider the same broad overstatement, but made in two ways that convey the same fact: English speaking children are so limited in their linguistic abilities that they must create a new strategy for each semantically different problem type — versus — LEP children must rely upon more primitive problem-solving strategies.

The reasons for choosing one or the other option have very little to do with the internal workings of psychology on the learning of mathematics. They have more to do with the assumptions and values that guide that psychology. To choose one or another option is to make tacit statements about the groups being considered. To create different models is to claim, tacitly, that there are some fundamental differences among the groups. To modify the existing description may be more parsimonious. However, unless the modification is done carefully, it may represent little more than a marginal statement about the populations at hand — that is, they may still be viewed as being fundamentally deviant.

The problem of accounting for discrepant academic performance among various groups as early as third grade, using results from the National Assessment of Educational Progress in Mathematics (NAEP), and maybe even sooner, remains unresolved. However, when we look to the children's mathematical thinking as the source of those discrepancies, we find competence of a sort that would not have been predicted. There still may be deficiencies of a particular kind at play, but the picture is more complicated than that. Moreover, the existence of such competence should raise the possibility that we might need to look elsewhere — other than in the area of student learning — in order to develop a complete account.

RESEARCH ON TEACHERS' THINKING WHILE
TEACHING MATHEMATICS

The research on teachers' thought processes while teaching mathematics is another example in which theoretical
models represent the validation of social arrangements.
During the past few years, we have moved from process-
product paradigms of research on teaching, in which
teachers were a black box to be told what to do or to be by-
passed in curriculum implementation (Romberg & Carpenter, 1986), to a view in which teachers are seen as thinking
beings who must make numerous and complicated decisions involving student learning, classroom management,
the flow of instruction and a host of other tasks. We have become very interested in how teachers make those sorts of
decisions, in their general beliefs about the nature of what
they teach, and in their attitudes and the sorts of knowledge that they must bring to bear in planning and implementing their lessons (Carpenter, Fennema, Peterson &
Carey, 1988; Clark & Peterson, 1986; Cobb, 1988; Lampert, 1986; Leinhardt, 1986; Peterson, et al., 1989; Stanic
& Reyes, 1986).

While the picture of teaching that comes out of this
work is not as well developed as for addition and subtraction, some themes are evolving. The good teacher is one who
has sophisticated knowledge of the mathematics content
being taught; who believes that mathematics is more than
the rote memorization of procedures and facts but is also
an evolving and generative form of conceptually based
knowledge; who helps children connect what they know to
that content; and who employs a variety of instructional
strategies in achieving instructional goals. Moreover, the
expert mathematics teacher seems to have routinized most
of the everyday administrative and managerial aspects of
his/her classroom.

Missing: Teachers' Thinking about Student Diversity

Two studies investigating the teaching of mathematics
have involved diverse student populations. Leinhardt's

(1986, 1988) work has been conducted in integrated or predominantly black city schools, from which she has drawn heterogeneous ability groups of children for further study: "eight second grade students attending an all-black, lower SES elementary city school ... [and] eleven fourth grade students in an integrated, lower SES elementary city school" (Leinhardt, 1988, 122). Lampert (1986) taught a "heterogeneous group of 28 fourth graders" (p. 316).

What is missing from their studies, and indeed from most similar accounts of teaching, is what teachers think, believe, and do as a function of their diverse student populations. Though it seems that teachers focus their planning and preparation times primarily on the content matter to be taught in their classrooms, "the largest percentage of teachers' reports of their interactive thoughts [are] concerned with the learner" (Clark & Peterson, 1986, p. 269). The nature of those thoughts may be quite general, such as "nobody was listening at all" (p. 269) or quite specific. Stanic and Reyes (1986) report that a black seventh-grade mathematics teacher engaged in differential and quite purposeful behavior toward his students as a function of student gender and race. The teacher was critical of a black male's academic efforts on the grounds that he did not try hard enough and was in danger of falling into the "black athlete syndrome." In contrast, the teacher was more encouraging and gave more latitude to a particular white male. With a black female he tended to be more social, though still encouraging in his interactions. With a white female, he responded to her requests for help but, otherwise, did not really engage her.

The literature on teaching is replete with instances of differential teacher behaviors toward students as a function of race, gender, class, language, or differential student ability (Grant, 1989). Some differential behaviors may be responses to initial student behaviors (Brophy, 1986; Stanic & Reyes, 1986). Others seem to be adaptive successful teaching strategies. Grant (1989) suggests that increased response wait time is needed to "explicitly inform" black males that they are "expected to be academically successful" (p. 9). Brophy and Good (1986) conclude that:

> It was especially essential for teachers in low-SES
> classes to monitor activity, supervise seatwork,
> and initiate interactions with students who
> needed help of supervision. Teachers in high-SES
> classes did not have to be quite so vigilant . . . Pos-
> itive affect, a relaxed learning climate, and praise
> for student responses were also more related to
> achievement in low-SES settings. (p. 349)

Moreover, the evidence also suggests that teachers have
differing beliefs about their students. Clark and Peterson
(1986) report effects of race and social class on teachers' attributions for student success and/or failure, but no such
effects based on student gender (p. 284). Grant (1989) reviews research in which teachers assign differential ability
to their students as a function of race and use of Black English Vernacular. Orr (1987), a practicing mathematics
teacher, writes eloquently about how teachers lower their
expectations of many black students due to their frustrations in teaching them. In contrast, those teachers change
their expectations when they discover, after challenging the
students to think about the mathematical language used
in algebra and geometry, that their students are capable of
more and better work. Baron, Tom, and Cooper (1985) review research that shows that teachers have differential expectations for the success of their students as functions of
race and class, but that these expectations are differentially
revealed as a function of the stimulus.

The link between teacher beliefs and thinking about
their diverse student populations on the one hand, and
their actual in-classroom decision making on the other,
seems to be unclear. Clark and Peterson (1986) could not
find any studies that specifically tied these two. The only
such study of which I am aware is Stanic and Reyes (1986).

In my own informal discussions with mathematics
teachers, I have come to believe that their decisions are influenced by their notions of efficiency and justice. For example, I visited an urban district in the Midwest that was
undergoing a series of initiatives for desegregation as well

as for the education of their increasing immigrant student population. The high school mathematics teachers were especially critical of anything associated with the program for their school's Limited English Proficient (LEP) students. I had to face their anger at being placed in a situation for which they were, frankly, unprepared. As one teacher put it, "I was trained to teach mathematics, not to teach *those* students." The teachers' comments also made it very clear that many of them would just as soon have nothing to do with their school's LEP student population. At a middle school, another teacher casually mentioned that there are many teachers who actually *enjoy* teaching *those* students; that they "even come willingly" to workshops and other forms of staff development on the topic. So, couldn't we arrange things so that those sorts of teachers got all of those students (so that the rest of us would not have to deal with them)?

Two high school teachers addressed the issue of allocation of personal resources very succinctly: "Why should I spend all of my time with one of those students, when 29 of our students need help? I could spend all of my time with just a few of them. They receive tutoring in their own language, when many of *our* students, who need the help just as much, don't. Why should I help them, when they're going to get the help anyway?"

These comments — and I have run into them throughout the Midwest — are not made by inexpert, beginning teachers. The increasing age of our teaching population (Center for Education Statistics, 1987a, 1987b), and many teachers' self-reports about their frustrations over their many years of teaching suggest that, if anything, these comments are being made by experienced, (possibly) overworked, teachers. They also reflect a wholesale rejection, by some teachers, of entire segments of their classrooms. Moreover, the last two comments suggest that teacher beliefs about the efficacy and/or the justice of attending to such populations find their way into their interactive classroom decisions, in the form of withholding resources from students.

Most of the research on teacher cognitions asks teachers to provide retrospective reports about why they performed as they did. These two comments suggest that as long as we ask teachers to explain *only* what they have done, we will not obtain as complete a picture as we might want of how teachers work in classrooms with diverse learners. We also need to find out why teachers *don't* do some things. For example, if two students raise their hands to seek help, to respond to a question, or to seek the teacher's attention in some other way, the teacher's decision to attend to one student is made at the expense of the other. The teacher must allocate the resources under his or her direct control —in this example, class and/or personal time.

The Legitimation of Expertise as a Social Arrangement

Certainly we need to open up the black box between the intended and the implemented curriculum. Key in that process is the teacher and his or her thoughts and decisions. On the other hand, the focus on mathematical content and pedagogical knowledge results in a picture of good teaching that is incomplete. It presents "expert" teachers at work, and implies that content and pedagogical knowledge is enough. It would be easy, if erroneous, to conclude that if we have good teaching with bad results (as Schoenfeld, 1988, illustrates) for specific populations, the flaw must lie within the populations, not in the teaching. Brophy's (1986) characterization of good teaching as something that proceeds at a brisk pace stands in direct opposition to Grant's (1989) observation that black males do not participate in lessons as a form of resistance and that a good teacher will use increased wait time as an explicit means of communicating the expectation that they should participate in the class. Whereas Brophy's statement is general, Grant's is contingent. Which of the two is seen as core says more about what our research has legitimated than it does about the facts.

Let us assume that the teachers I have been running into have the kind of knowledge and beliefs outlined by Carpenter and his associates (Carpenter, et al., 1989; Peterson, et al., 1989), Lampert (1986) and Leinhardt (1988). Let us even assume that they are expert in implementing instructional and social arrangements that have been shown to enhance student achievement in general. What is still missing is those teachers' knowledge and beliefs about their students. If they withhold instruction, even if they try to treat every student equally (the tacit ideal in many dyadic interaction studies, as well as an ideal expressed by many teachers), it is far from obvious that they will be treating their students in a just manner. Fennema and Peterson (1987) and Stanic and Reyes (1986) provide additional examples of how equal treatment in the mathematics classroom can result in unequal outcomes based on student gender and race.

What role might teacher beliefs and knowledge about students, as functions of gender, race, ethnicity, language, and social class, serve? We know from the literature that good teachers establish routines and resolve most managerial tasks early during the school year (Brophy, 1986; Doyle, 1986), during which time, instruction must still proceed. Another characteristic of good teachers is that they try to pitch instruction to match and extend children's levels of thinking. Hence, student demographic characteristics may serve as proxies for student ability during the start of the school year; after all, teachers have received ample information concerning the academic achievement disparities among these various groups. While they are otherwise engaged in establishing the routines of their classrooms, teachers communicate these expectations to their students who, by the time the teacher gets around to gathering direct information about ability, have proceeded to live up or down to those expectations. At this time, those expectations receive validation.

Some evidence supporting this hypothesis comes from a review by Raudebush (cited in Rosenthal, 1987) in which teacher expectancies were found to be more malleable when they had known their children less than (as opposed to more than) two weeks. Cognitively Guided Instruction (CGI) provides some interesting possibilities as a means of

incorporating student diversity into models of teacher cognition (Carpenter, et al., 1989). One of the strongest outcomes of that study was that teachers were empowered with
a means for obtaining direct evidence concerning student
cognition early on during the academic year. Fennema (personal communication) has noted that teachers in the experimental group, who received training on CGI during its
first year, were no different from controls in their ability to
predict how boys would do on solving arithmetic word problems; yet they were better than controls in predicting how
girls would perform. Moreover, experimental teachers
seemed to engage in less gender-stereotypical behaviors involving girls than their comparison peers. Finally, though
no differences were found between classes of children on
the solving of simple word problems at posttest, students in
the control group showed the classic pattern of growth in
which pretest scores predicted posttest achievement. For
the experimental group, however, the regression line reported by Carpenter, et al. (1989) was almost horizontal,
that is, pretest performance did *not* predict posttest performance. Dampening the predictive ability of very early
achievement on later success has been one of the most salient goals of compensatory education (Coleman, 1975); it
remains to be seen if CGI can help dampen the predictive
ability of other demographic factors as well.

I would caution against studying only more experienced
teachers, at least in middle and high school. There is a
strong folklore that students who are stratified into slower
classes or lower tracks (which are overpopulated by minority and low-SES students) typically receive their instruction from beginning or less senior teachers, while the more
experienced teachers successfully vie for more advanced
classes comprised of students considered easier to teach. It
is ironic and of questionable value to students that, as
teachers become more experienced and expert, they are re-
warded in this manner. It is as if beginning teachers hone
their craft on students who have been written off and,
hence, who will not be damaged by their inexpertise. How
such a career ladder affects a beginning mathematics

teacher's beliefs about disadvantaged students remains an open question.

If we consider the links between teachers' beliefs about students and their in-class decision making in terms of how teachers allocate the resources under their control, we can begin to ask questions about the social arrangements that such allocations represent. We can also investigate teachers' underlying conceptions of justice within such a conception: Do they try to give each student the same amount, or do they engage in purposeful differential allocation of attention, etc.? Also, there might be a relationship between resource allocation and the concentration of different kinds of students in the classroom. If a class contains one or two students who are perceived as "at risk," "problematic," or in some other sense "marginal," will teachers behave differently than if 30 to 40 percent of the classroom fits this description?

Teachers' pedagogical knowledge and beliefs may be quite similar. But, unless we know more about how pedagogy fits diverse student populations, we have knowledge that legitimates the status quo. If the current mathematics education of many groups of students represents an unjust social arrangement, then that continued legitimation is at best suspect.

AT THE INTERSECTION OF TEACHING AND LEARNING

It has become much in vogue to write about the work that we expect students to engage in, even if we do call it academic (Doyle, 1983, 1988; Tomlinson & Walberg, 1986) and even if we are appalled when we read about schools that pay their students to participate in that work. There are efforts to characterize the tasks that students must fulfill if they are to learn mathematics (Doyle, 1988; Leinhardt & Putnam, 1987) and to tie classroom instruction to changes in children's thinking (Leinhardt, 1988). Leinhardt and Putnam (1987) lay out a comprehensive model of the learner that includes as components an action system, information gatherer, lesson parser, knowledge generator, and evaluator. This system is particularly intriguing since it provides some very specific mechanisms by which children could tie new information to preexisting knowledge in the context of classroom instruction.

Tacit in Doyle's analyses of classroom work and in Leinhardt and Putnam's model of the learner, however, is the assumption that all the children are seeking the same goals from the lesson; hence the students' beliefs about their classrooms, lessons and even the nature of meaningful work is omitted from their model. Leinhardt (1988), for example, describes Chuck, a second-grade student who "operated in a mild cloud of faith. If the teacher told him something, it was 'good' and for his benefit" (p. 130). The operation of Chuck's system is likely to look radically different from that of the older black male described by Grant (1989) who "often sees school as hostile to his welfare, and may see the teacher as a person who is out to get him" (p. 9). Each student is likely to be seeking different kinds of information from his lesson, and — assuming their integrated knowledge acquiring systems are intact — will impose radically different meanings on the lessons.

Is Academic Work Culture Free?

Another concern with Doyle's (1983, 1988) descriptions of academic work and with Leinhardt and Putnam's (1987) model of the learner is their silence about the cultural nature of the tasks that comprise academic work. Lily Wong Fillmore (1987, verbal communication) reviewed research involving diverse cultural styles of child rearing in terms of how children are socialized vis-à-vis work. According to Fillmore, children raised in traditional Hispanic households are given relatively large tasks to manage. These include taking care of younger siblings, setting the table, or helping with the cooking and cleaning. They are expected to try tasks, even if they don't get them right. It is understood that a large task may be too difficult but that, with help and over time, the child will get closer and closer to mastery. The task is meaningful in that it is well situated within the child's home environment, and adultlike. In the

Hispanic culture, the stress is placed on the child's maturity in picking up and in mastering such adultlike tasks. For example, though parents supervise their children, it is not uncommon to hear older children refer to younger siblings as "my baby," and for the older to serve as a protector and parent surrogate for the younger sibling.

In traditional Chinese culture, on the other hand, child rearing places great stress on the child's level of accomplishment within small tasks that adults assign and monitor. Chinese children are expected to master these tasks before they move on to other, larger, more adultlike, and (in Fillmore's terms) more meaningful tasks. For example, a Chinese child will be told to keep his or her sibling from doing a specific thing, to set a small part of the table, to pick up a specific item. In all cases, the task is very local, always adult guided, and it is clear that the adult is in charge.

Finally, among traditional American Indians, the stress in child rearing seems to be on developing the singular authority of the individual to determine his or her own direction. Parents do not explicitly assign tasks, rather the child is expected to select tasks from the range of adult behaviors he or she observes. The child learns the facets of the task by observing how it is performed by those who engage in it, and he or she practices the task in private until it is ready for public display. Unlike Hispanic and Chinese parents, Indian parents do not ask for a display of what is being learned; rather, the child determines when something is finished enough to be placed on public display.

The sorts of praise that children receive as a function of task mastery also seems to vary. Hispanic parents will acknowledge their children's efforts, as long as they tried hard. The child's maturity for being so independent in trying such a hard task is noted, and the contingency is that the attempt be better executed next time. Chinese parents, on the other hand, do not seem to acknowledge successful mastery of a task, though they will comment when the task has not been well done. After all, the task was pitched well within the child's reach and was executed under adult guidance. Acknowledgement of their children's efforts by American Indian parents seems muted; again, this seems tied to the belief of the child as the authority for what he or she does. On the other hand, there is considerable teasing — a form of acknowledgement — within groups of children to prevent anyone from getting a swollen head.

Fillmore then applied her analysis to observations of Hispanic and Chinese children in first-grade arithmetic. Children were told to write as many numbers as they could on a piece of paper. The Chinese children competed with themselves, individually, and with each other to see who could fit the most numbers on the page. Their writing became smaller and smaller in an effort to fit as many numbers as possible on the sheet of paper. On the other hand, the Hispanic children did the task but did not try to go beyond it as did their Chinese peers. The Hispanic children seemed to see this as a very direct assignment with no meaning attached to it beyond its completion. People familiar with currently used arithmetic curricula would likely agree with Fillmore's observation that, as designed and implemented, it is replete with such small tasks that can be disposed of without having to attend to its deeper meanings.

The Display of Competence

The issue of school tasks as appropriate for displays of knowledge by traditional American Indian children becomes critical. Deyhle (1987) documents how Anglo children, as early as second grade, understand that tests are tasks on which one displays knowledge and that these displays matter in terms of the school's culture. On the other hand, it was not until fourth grade that Navajo children began to consistently recognize the central roles that tests were meant to play in the lives of their classrooms. Until that time, they considered tests to be just another of the many events in which they were expected to participate. Deyhle (1987) notes:

> When Navajo children enter school, they come with a culturally determined understanding of the appropriate means of displaying competence.

This is different from the processes required in school — demonstrating individual knowledge through public display (classroom questioning) or through testing ... Teacher frustration focused upon the students' apparent lack of respect, acceptance or understanding of personal failure on tests. The teachers assumed that because the students did not approach testing seriously or respond with remorse when they received poor grades, they were not serious or motivated about learning in general. This was the teachers' way of putting the blame for their academic failure on the students ... In the home, Navajo children learned without the public, individual displays of knowledge. These children, therefore, entered school without an understanding that the school was going to require them to learn via questions and tests—through a constant and public display of mistakes and failure. (pp. 105–106)

Cultural Mismatch versus Tacit Relations of Power

The cultural mismatch between children and school (arithmetic in particular) on how meaningful and how large tasks are, the expectations for work conditions and for success, the conditions under which task competence should be demonstrated, and the rewards that are given as a function of success may be a source of the disparate learning and achievement experienced by many ethnic minorities in mathematics. Neither Doyle's (1983, 1988) nor Leinhardt and Putnam's (1987) discussions of the tasks involved in learning in the classroom allow for differential student perceptions about the value of the task in which they are being asked to engage:

A lack of structure in a lesson or a mismatch between the structure of an actual lesson and the structure of the learner's lesson schema can cause considerable difficulty for the lesson parser ... For example, a novice teacher's lesson that does not make use of routines and lesson seg-

> ments ... can result in confusion on the part of
> the students. If a student has not developed the
> capability of parsing a lesson, he or she may get
> lost frequently or find following lessons a demand-
> ing task. (Leinhardt & Putnam, 1987, p. 567)

Missing is the notion that not only might the structures be problematic, but their actual contents might also be as well.

As is common in much psychological work, the re-search at the intersection of teaching and learning of math-ematics tries to remain neutral on the disparate kinds of knowledge that children bring to school with them. Yet the tasks for the learner as described by Doyle and Leinhardt are not value free. They must be aligned to the socially and culturally determined expectations that children bring with them about what is meaningful in school.

The issue is how to research that differential knowledge and expectation base. Leinhardt (1988) notes that Chuck, "a marginal student ... flourished because of considerable care on the part of his teacher" (p. 128). Fennema (personal communication) has spoken repeatedly of how teachers in-volved in Cognitively Guided Instruction adjust their inter-actions with students to account for what the children ac-tually can do, maybe with a little help. Their response accommodates individual differences; it is to be lauded. Yet as long as we look only for responses based on individual differences, we are still in danger of treating these chil-dren's knowledge as marginal and of not really addressing the privileged status of school-based knowledge. Individual differences are tied to culture, class, gender, ethnicity, and language.

For example, Leinhardt's line of research seems to be leading to a mapping of changes in student cognition, mod-eled through semantic nets, as a function of teaching. The desired end point seems to be a student network of knowl-edge that closely matches that of the expert teacher's. In other words, the teacher's knowledge is the more valued and she/he is also the more powerful. Both of these features bear further investigation from the perspective of how stu-dents react to lessons: An older Chuck may have stopped trusting his teacher and, in fact, may have actively resisted his/her efforts at teaching. The models of the learner being proposed by current work at the intersection of teaching and learning mathematics would not be able to give an account of why this happens.

CONCLUSIONS

I began this paper by questioning the equity of research that excludes student diversity from its concerns. In the first part of this paper, I was concerned with the sorts of social arrangements that find legitimation through the exclusion of such populations. All three domains — learning, teaching, and teaching/learning — share the exclusion of these groups from their efforts and the tacit claim of being somehow neutral and generally applicable. For each of these three, I tried to review some research that makes plausible the claim that these efforts, while coherent, are incomplete.

A danger in conducting this kind of research lies in the stress placed upon the individual and the submerging of that individual's race, social class, gender, and other characteristics that locate that individual as a member of our society and of groups within that society. By excluding characteristics of diversity, we can create technically sophisticated models of the learning and teaching of mathematics. Tacit claims of universal applicability, however, must be tempered by the degree to which this research transforms problems of affect, course taking, underachievement, and careers into problems within the individual. Since cognitivist models of learning and teaching are seen as universally applicable to individuals, deviance from those models is interpreted as being due to individual differences. The alternative, that such differences are a function of the individual's membership in a social group and that said membership is constructed through a complex web of social forces, cannot be addressed at present. We are in danger of creating models that further legitimate the characterization of minority students, who are becoming an increasingly larger portion of our population, as deficient.

An alternative naturally arises. At its best, purest or otherwise, can cognitive science create universally applicable models of human cognition? If so, then my objections would tend to fade, since in that sense, its information would be basic. For example, we all certainly agree that how students understand arithmetic word problems is the foundation for the way they solve them.

We must unpack claims of neutrality or universality in terms of their specific meanings. *Understanding* is one such term that is fraught with social, cultural, and other meanings. In cognitivist terms, understanding is based on information-processing notions of the mind that are modeled through the use of flow charts, semantic networks, or contingency-based production systems. Since I have not seen any efforts that specifically demonstrate how membership in diverse groups can be addressed, this remains an open and empirical issue. On the other hand, the models of human information processing that I have seen constrain our interpretations of divergent forms of thinking, as inferred from behaviors and self-reports, to one of two conclusions: Either something is missing from the processing system (there is a hole in the flow chart) or the system is not as mature as another (a less elaborated flow chart is at work).

In conclusion, current research on the teaching and learning of mathematics contains elements that serve to legitimate views of diverse learners as deficient learners. It also may contain the promise of helping us assess when deficiency is, in fact, an issue, versus those cases when the legitimation of social arrangements are at work. As long as this research continues to exclude diversity from its concerns, and as long as what has been developed with one population is transferred to apply to another, the former will be the case.

If I could make one recommendation, it would be this: Our research needs to become broader in its scope. It is not enough to research children's cognitions, unless we address how divergent forms of cognition can develop in a manner that does not marginalize those forms. Work on teaching, while attending to teacher beliefs, knowledge, and behaviors in terms of content knowledge, needs to expand to include teacher beliefs, knowledge, and behaviors as a function of the sorts of students who are in their classrooms. And research at the intersection of teaching and learning needs to include both points.

By its silence on the kinds of competence that diverse student populations bring to the mathematics classroom, research legitimates that they are deviant. By its silence on how teachers interact with these students, it legitimates the ignoring of important social and cultural differences. Insofar as research legitimates such arrangements that are inherently unjust, then a concern for equity would argue that the research needs to be expanded.

REFERENCES

Aristotle. (1981). *Rhetoric* (Translated by W. Rhys Roberts). Philadelphia: Franklin Institute Press. [Reprinted from *The works of Aristotle*. Oxford: Oxford University Press.]

Baron, R. M., Tom, D. Y. H., & Cooper, H. M. (1985). Social class, race and teacher expectations. In J. B. Dusek (Ed.), *Teacher expectancies* (pp. 251–269). Hillsdale, NJ: Lawrence Erlbaum Associates.

Ben-Zeev, S. (1977). The influence of bilingualism on cognitive strategy and cognitive development. *Child Development, 48,* 1009–1018.

Broadbent, F. W., & Daniele, V. A. (1982). A review of research on mathematics and deafness. *Directions, 3,* 27–36.

Brophy, J. (1986). Teaching and learning mathematics: Where research should be going. *Journal for Research in Mathematics Education, 17*(5), 323–346.

Brophy, J., & Good, T. L. (1986). Teacher behavior and student achievement. In M. C. Wittrock (Ed.), *Handbook of research on teaching* (3rd ed., pp. 328–375). New York: Macmillan.

Campbell, P. B. (1989). Educational equity and research paradigms. In W. G. Secada (Ed.), *Equity in education* (pp. 26–42). London: Falmer Press.

Carpenter, T. P., Fennema, E., Peterson, P. L., & Carey, D. A. (1988). Teachers' pedagogical content knowledge of students' problem solving in elementary arithmetic. *Journal for Research in Mathematics Education, 19*(5), 385–401.

Carpenter, T. P., Fennema, E., Peterson, P. L., Chiang, C., & Loef, M. (1989). Using knowledge of children's mathematical thinking in classroom teaching: An experimental study. *American Educational Research Journal, 26*(4), 499–532.

Carpenter, T. P., & Moser, J. M. (1983). The acquisition of addition and subtraction concepts. In R. Lesh & M. Landau (Eds.), *The acquisition of mathematical concepts and processes* (pp. 7–44). New York: Academic Press.

Center for Education Statistics. (1987a). *The condition of education.* Washington, DC: Government Printing Office.

———. (1987b). *Digest of education statistics.* Washington, DC: Government Printing Office.

Clark, C. M., & Peterson, P. L. (1986). Teachers' thought processes. In M. C. Wittrock (Ed.), *Handbook of research on teaching* (3rd ed., pp. 255–296). New York: Macmillan.

Cobb, P. (1988). The tension between theories of learning and instruction in mathematics education. *Educational Psychologist* (Learning from instruction: The study of students' thinking during instruction in mathematics. Special issue.), *23*(2), 87–103.

Cole, M., & Griffin, P. (Eds.) (1987). *Contextual factors in education: Improving science and mathematics education for minorities and women.* Wisconsin Center for Education Research, University of Wisconsin-Madison.

Coleman, J. (1975). What is meant by an 'equal educational opportunity?' *Oxford Review of Education, 1*(1), 27–29.

Crandall, J., Dale, T. C., Rhodes, N. C., & Spanos, G. (1987). *English language skills for basic algebra.* Englewood Cliffs, NJ: Prentice Hall.

———. (in press). The language of mathematics: The English barrier. *Proceedings of the 1985 Delaware Symposium on Language Studies* (VII). Newark, DE: University of Delaware Press.

Cuevas, G. (1984). Mathematical learning in English as a second language. *Journal for Research in Mathematics Education, 15*, 134–144.

De Avila, E. A., & Duncan, S. E. (1981). *A convergent approach to language assessment* (Stock 621). San Rafael, CA: Linguametrics.

De Corte, E., & Verschaffel, L. (1987). The effect of semantic structure on first graders' strategies for solving addition and subtraction word problems. *Journal for Research in Mathematics Education, 18*(5), 363–381.

Deyhle, D. (1987). Learning failure: Tests as gatekeepers and the culturally different child. In H. T. Trueba (Ed.), *Success or failure? Learning and the language minority child* (pp. 85–108). Cambridge, MA: Newbury House.

Diaz, R. M. (1983). Thought and two languages: The impact of bilingualism on cognitive development. *Review of Research in Education, 10,* 23–54.

Doyle, W. (1983). Academic work. *Review of Educational Research, 53,* 159–199.

———. (1986). Classroom organization and management. In M. C. Wittrock (Ed.), *Handbook of research on teaching* (3rd ed., pp. 392–431). New York: Macmillan.

———. (1988). Work in mathematics classes: The content of students' thinking during instruction. *Educational Psychologist* (Learning from instruction: The study of students' thinking during instruction in mathematics. Special issue.), *23*(2), 167–180.

Duran, R. P. (1988). Bilinguals' logical reasoning ability: A construct validity study. In R. R. Cocking & J. P. Mestre (Eds.), *Linguistic and cultural influences on learning mathematics* (pp. 241–258). Hillsdale, NJ: Lawrence Erlbaum Associates.

Educational Researcher (1986, June/July). The new scholarship on women (Special issue), *15*(6).

Fennema, E., & Peterson, P. L. (1987). Effective teaching for girls and boys: The same or different? In D. C. Berliner & B. V. Rosenshine (Eds.), *Talks to teachers* (pp. 111–125). New York: Random House.

Fillmore, L. W. (1987, September 24). *Is effective teaching equally effective across diverse cultural learning styles?* Presentation made at a Symposium Sponsored by the Upper Great Lakes Multifunctional Resource Center, University of Wisconsin-Madison.

Fuson, K. C. (1988). *Children's counting and concepts of number.* New York: Springer-Verlag.

Gelman, R. (1978). Cognitive development. *Annual Review of Psychology, 29,* 297–332.

Grant, C. A. (1989). Equity, equality, teachers and classroom life. In W. G. Secada (Ed.), *Equity in education* (pp. 89–102). London: Falmer Press.

Ianco-Worrall, D. A. (1972). Bilingualism and cognitive development. *Child Development, 43*, 1390–1400.

Kallos, D., & Lundgren, U. P. (1975). Educational psychology: Its scope and limits. *British Journal of Educational Psychology, 45*, 111–121.

Kintsch, W., & Greeno, J. G. (1985). Understanding and solving arithmetic word problems. *Psychology Review, 92*(1), 109–129.

Lampert, M. (1986). Knowing, doing, and teaching multiplication. *Cognition and Instruction, 3*(4), 305–342.

Leinhardt, G. (1986). Expertise in mathematics teaching. *Educational Leadership, 43*(7), 28–33.

———. (1988). Getting to know: Tracing students' mathematical knowledge from intuition to competence. *Educational Psychologist* (Learning through instruction: The study of students' thinking during instruction in mathematics. Special issue.), *23*(2), 119–144.

Leinhardt, G., & Putnam, R. (1987). The skill of learning from classroom lessons. *American Educational Research Journal, 24*(4), 557–587.

McDowell, G. L. (1981). *Equity and the Constitution.* Chicago: University of Chicago Press.

McLaughlin, B. (1986). *Second language acquisition in childhood.* Hillsdale, NJ: Lawrence Erlbaum Associates.

McLeod, D. B. (1988, May). *Research on learning and instruction in mathematics: The role of affect.* Paper presented at the First Wisconsin Symposium for Research on Teaching and Learning Mathematics, Madison.

Mestre, J. (1988). The role of language comprehension in mathematics problem solving. In R. R. Cocking & J. P. Mestre (Eds.), *Linguistic and cultural influences on learning mathematics* (pp. 201–220). Hillsdale, NJ: Lawrence Erlbaum Associates.

Moores, D. (1976). Review of research in education of the hearing impaired. In L. Mann & D. Sabatino (Eds.), *Third review of special education* (pp. 17–57). Boston: Houghton Mifflin.

———. (1978). *Educating the deaf: Psychology, principles and practices* (2nd ed.). Boston: Houghton Mifflin. [2nd ed.]

Myklebust, H. (1964). *The psychology of deafness.* New York: Grune & Stratton.

Nesher, P. (1982). Levels of description in the analysis of addition and subtraction. In T. P. Carpenter, J. M. Moser, & T. A. Romberg (Eds.), *Addition and subtraction: A cognitive perspective* (pp. 25–38). Hillsdale, NJ: Lawrence Erlbaum Associates.

Oakes, J. (1987). *Opportunities, achievement, and choice: Issues in the participation of women, minorities and the disabled in science* (Paper prepared for the National Science Foundation). Santa Monica, CA: Rand.

————. (in press). The distribution of excellence: Indicators of equity in precollege mathematics, science and technology education. To appear in R. Shavelson, L. McDonnell, & J. Oakes (Eds.), *Indicators of math and science education: A source book*. Santa Monica, CA: Rand.

Ogbu, J. U. (1978). *Minority education and caste: The American system in cross-cultural perspective*. Orlando, FL: Academic Press.

Ogbu, J. U., & Matute-Bianchi, M. E. (1986). Understanding sociological factors: Knowledge, identity, and school adjustment. In Bilingual Education Office, CA Department of Education, *Beyond language: Social and cultural factors in schooling language minority students* (pp. 73–142). Los Angeles: Evaluation, Dissemination and Assessment Center, CA State University.

Orr, E. W. (1987). *Twice as less: Black English and the performance of black students in mathematics and science*. New York: Basic Books.

Padilla, A. M. (1988, April). *Around the turn and into the 21st century: New perspectives on bilingual education*. Paper presented at the Annual Meeting of the American Educational Research Association, New Orleans, LA.

Peterson, P. L., Fennema, E., Carpenter, T. P., & Loef, M. (1989). Teachers' pedagogical content beliefs in mathematics. *Cognition and Instruction, 6*(1), 1–40.

Popkewitz, T. S. (1984). *Paradigm and ideology in educational research: The social function of the intellectual*. London: Falmer Press.

————. (1986). Paradigm and purpose. In C. Cornbleth (Ed.), *An invitation to research in social education* (Bulletin No. 77, pp. 10–27). Washington, DC: National Council for the Social Studies.

Re, E. D. (1982). *Remedies: Cases and materials* (University Casebook Series). Mineola, NY: The Foundation Press, Inc.

Resnick, L. B., & Ford, W. W. (1981). *The psychology of mathematics for instruction*. Hillsdale, NJ: Erlbaum.

Romberg, T. A., & Carpenter, T. P. (1986). Research on teaching and learning mathematics: Two disciplines of inquiry. In M. C. Wittrock (Ed.), *Handbook of research on teaching* (3rd ed., pp. 850–873). New York: Macmillan.

Rosenthal, R. (1987). Pygmalion effect: Existence, magnitude and social importance. *Educational Researcher, 16*(9), 37–41.

Sampson, E. E. (1977). Psychology and the American ideal. *Journal of Personality and Social Psychology, 35*(11), 767–782.

———. (1981). Cognitive psychology as ideology. *American Psychologist, 36*(7), 730–743.

Saxe, G. (1988). Linking language with mathematics achievement: Problems and prospects. In R. R. Cocking & J. P. Mestre (Eds.), *Linguistic and cultural influences on learning mathematics* (pp. 47–62). Hillsdale, NJ: Lawrence Erlbaum Associates.

Schoenfeld, A. H. (1988). When good teaching leads to bad results: The disasters of "well taught" mathematic courses. *Educational Psychologist* (Learning from instruction: The study of students' thinking during instruction in mathematics. Special issue.), *23*(2) 145–166.

Secada, W. G. (1982, March). *The use of counting by manually trained deaf children for addition and subtraction*. Paper presented at the Meeting of the American Educational Research Association, New York.

———. (1988). Watching our language (Narrative review of *Twice as less* by Eleanor Wilson Orr and *Speaking mathematically* by David Pimm). *Journal for Research in Mathematics Education, 19*(4), 362–366.

———. (1989a). Educational equity versus equality of education: An alternative conception. In W. G. Secada (Ed.), *Equity in education* (pp. 68–88). London: Falmer Press.

———. (Ed.). (1989b). *Equity in education*. London: Falmer.

———. (1990). Student diversity in mathematics education reform. In L. Idol & B. F. Jone (Eds.), *Dimensions in thinking and cognitive instruction* (pp. 295–330). Hillsdale, NJ: Lawrence Erlbaum Associates.

———. (in press). Degree of bilingualism and arithmetic problem-solving in Hispanic first graders. *Elementary School Journal*.

Spanos, G., Rhodes, N. C., Dale, T. C., & Crandall, J. (1988). Linguistic features of mathematical problem solving: Insights and applications. In R. R. Cocking & J. P. Mestre (Eds.), *Linguistic and cultural influences on learning mathematics* (pp. 221 – 240). Hillsdale, NJ: Lawrence Erlbaum Associates.

Stanic, G. M. A., & Reyes, L. H. (1986, April). *Gender and race differences in mathematics: A case study of a seventh grade classroom.* Paper presented at the Meeting of the American Educational Research Association, San Francisco.

Tomlinson, T. M., & Walberg, H. J. (Eds.). (1986). *Academic work and educational excellence: Raising student productivity.* Berkeley, CA: McCutchan.

Zentella, A. C. (1981). Ta' bien. You could answer me en cualquier idioma: Puerto Rican codeswitching in bilingual classrooms. In R. Duran (Ed.), *Latino language and communicative behavior* (pp. 109–131). Norwood, NJ: Ablex.

———. (1987, December). *A sociolinguistic perspective on bilingualism.* Presentation made at the Harvard Institute on Bilingual Education: Research to Policy to Practice, Cambridge, MA.

3

Research on Learning and Instruction in Mathematics: The Role of Affect*

Douglas B. McLeod

Affective factors play a central role in mathematics learning and instruction. When you talk with teachers about how their mathematics classes are doing, they seem just as likely to mention the affective climate in the classroom as to report the cognitive achievements of their students. Similarly, inquiries of students are just as likely to produce affective as cognitive responses. Based on these informal observations, it seems reasonable to postulate that affect plays a significant role in learning and instruction. Although affect appears to play a central role in the lives of students and teachers, research on affect in mathematics education continues to reside on the periphery of the field. If research on learning and instruction is to maximize its impact on students and teachers, affective factors need to occupy a more central position in the minds of researchers.

The role of affect as a central issue in mathematics education has been reaffirmed in the recent publication of the standards for curriculum and evaluation by the National Council of Teachers of Mathematics (Commission on Stan-

---

*Preparation of this paper was supported in part by National Science Foundation Grant No. MDR-8696142. Any opinions, conclusions, or recommendations are those of the author and do not necessarily reflect the views of the National Science Foundation.

55

dards for School Mathematics, 1989). Two of the major goals stated in this document deal with helping students understand the value of mathematics and with developing student confidence. In its Standard on mathematical disposition, the assessment of student confidence, interest, perseverance, and curiosity are all recommended. Although the Standards document places considerable importance on affective issues, it does not attempt to present a theoretical framework for the assessment of affect.

The purpose of this paper is to present a new approach to research on affect, and to indicate how affect can be incorporated into current mathematics education research efforts. The paper first discusses some psychological theories that have had an impact on research related to affect and mathematics education, and then presents a framework for research on affect that is compatible with current cognitive approaches to learning and instruction. Next, the paper summarizes a number of new studies of learners and teachers that do include affect as a major factor. Finally, the paper explores how an integrated view of affect and cognition might inform current models of research on learning and instruction, and comments specifically on the Cognitively Guided Instruction model of Carpenter and Fennema (1988).

The term *affect* in this discussion is used to refer to a wide range of beliefs, feelings, and moods that are generally regarded as going beyond the domain of cognition. In the context of mathematics education, these feelings and moods are often described with words like anxiety, confidence, frustration, and satisfaction. Frequently these feelings are discussed in the literature as *attitudes,* although that term does not seem adequate to describe some of the more intense emotional reactions that occur in mathematics classrooms. For example, the "Aha!" experience in mathematical problem solving is generally recognized as a joyful event, one that does not fit traditional definitions of attitudes. Later in this paper, beliefs, emotions, and attitudes will be used to describe the affective domain. For further discussion of the meaning of the terms, especially their different uses in psychology and mathematics education, see the work of Hart (1989) and Simon (1982).

PSYCHOLOGICAL THEORIES AND AFFECT

Changes in psychological theories have had a major impact on how affect is treated in mathematics education research. Frequently researchers have treated affect as an avoidable complication of modest significance; students have been viewed in rather mechanistic terms. This inadequate view of students is often related to the weaknesses of certain research paradigms in psychology.

The influence of behaviorism on educational psychology in this century has been an important factor in the neglect of the affective domain. Skinner (1953), for example, described the emotions as examples of imaginary constructs that were commonly used as causes of behavior. Mandler (1985) indicated some of the reasons that behaviorists were often unwilling to look closely at the influence of affective factors on learners.

The behaviorist view generally ignored the emotions, but it has been a major influence on the development of research on attitude in social psychology (Azjen & Fishbein, 1980). Leder's (1987) recent review of research on attitudes toward mathematics reflects the influence of this same behaviorist position, as well as the influences of differential psychology. The emphasis in both of these research traditions tends to be on using questionnaires to measure attitudes and to look at the correlations between these attitude scores and behavior. Such an approach has not been highly successful, and experts in the fields of psychology (Abelson, 1976; Mandler, 1972) and mathematics education (Kulm, 1980) have noted the need for better theory to guide research on this topic.

Freudian psychology has certainly recognized the importance of the emotions, but little of the psychoanalytic research has touched directly on issues that are central to

mathematics education. There are some exceptions, however. Nimier (1977), in an intriguing discussion of the impact of fears and defense mechanisms on mathematics students, provided a Freudian interpretation of certain
patterns of behavior that are common in mathematics
classrooms. In related work, Ligault (1987) discussed how
these Freudian interpretations of student behavior have
special implications for gender differences in mathematics
education. Although these studies have not yet had a major
impact on mathematics learning, they bring the techniques of depth psychology to the analysis of affective factors in mathematics education. Such techniques may in
the future yield important insights, especially for students
with extremely negative reactions to mathematics.

Developmental psychology also appears to have little to
say about the role of affect in mathematics learning. As
Bearison and Zimilies (1986) suggested, research on the
development of cognitive and affective domains is not well
connected. The difficulties can be traced back to Piaget
(1981), who argued that the cognitive and affective domains were inseparable but also different in nature. As
Sigel (1986) noted, Piaget resolved the difficulties by generally ignoring affect in his research, and concentrating instead on issues related to moral development. Although
some researchers have taken a more serious look at how the
emotions develop among young children (Kagan, 1978;
Skemp, 1979), the dominant view has been one of benign
neglect.

The constructivist researchers in mathematics education have generally followed developmental psychology's approach of ignoring affect, but this pattern has begun to
change. For example, von Glasersfeld (1987) noted the powerful positive emotions that often go along with the construction of new ideas or the cognitive reorganization of old
ideas. Similarly, Cobb (1985) has written of the importance
of confidence and willingness to persist as students develop
mathematical concepts. The constructivists do not generally give a high priority to the study of affective factors in
mathematics learning, but their commitment to using

qualitative methods does make it possible for them to observe and report the influence of affect on learners.

Perhaps the most productive research area in recent years has been the study of causal attributions (Weiner, 1986) and the application of these ideas to the study of motivation and emotion. This approach has been particularly fruitful in the analysis of gender differences in the learning of mathematics. Work by Fennema and Peterson (1985), Kloosterman (1988), and Reyes (1984) has been quite successful in clarifying how attributions of success and failure can lead to differences in mathematical performance. Although there have been some attempts to coordinate this approach with cognitive theories (Frieze, 1976; Weiner, 1982), generally the work on causal attributions has proceeded on a separate track from cognitively-oriented research on learning and instruction.

The emerging discipline of cognitive science has been rather slow to take affective factors into account. Gardner (1985) noted that cognitive science has generally avoided complicating factors like affective and cultural issues in an attempt to simplify the research tasks. If cognitive science is concerned only about producing knowledge, that approach is a reasonable one to take. However, those who would argue that cognitive science has applications to mathematics education must also show that this approach has implications for real students and teachers, including the affective dimensions of learning and instruction.

In their efforts to show the applicability of their new discipline, several cognitive scientists have indicated how affective factors could be included in their theories. Norman (1981), for example, has outlined twelve issues, including emotions and belief systems, that deserve more attention in cognitive science, and suggested ways to connect these affective factors in cognitive models of learners. Although Norman's recognition of the importance of affective issues in cognitive science was a significant event for the field, it was not the first time that the issue was raised. Simon (1967), in an early defense of information-processing psychology, noted the importance of expanding the theory to include motivational and emotional factors; he also made a suggestion regarding how interruptions of plans might be the mechanism that would trigger emotional reactions. The ideas behind this suggestion continue to be influential in more current theories of affect that come from the perspective of cognitive science.

Those who have investigated the applicability of cognitive science and its methodology to research in mathematics education have frequently noted that cognitive theories need to pay attention to more than just pure cognition. Schoenfeld (1985) and Silver (1985) each have made a strong case for the importance of beliefs and affect in research on problem solving, and their argument can also be applied more generally to the teaching and learning of mathematics.

The methods as well as the concepts of cognitive theories have important implications for research on affect in mathematics education. As Schoenfeld (1987) points out, cognitive approaches tend to focus on the processes rather than the products of learning and instruction. This emphasis on process needs to be carried over to the affective domain. In the past, the study of affect has generally followed the paradigm of differential psychology, concentrating on issues of instrumentation and correlations of scores, often with far too little attention to theoretical issues (Mandler, 1972). It seems appropriate for the moment, at least, to concentrate instead on the development of theory rather than the development of instruments, and to focus on affective processes as well as products. These changes in outlook should help us develop a theoretical framework for affect that is coordinated with and contributes to a cognitively-guided approach to research on learning and instruction.

COGNITIVE APPROACHES TO RESEARCH ON AFFECT

The emergence of affect as an important part of cognitive theories has been documented recently by Snow and Farr (1987). Since Snow and Farr are interested in the improvement of learning and instruction, it is natural for them to pay serious attention to the affective domain. The beginning of these attempts to incorporate affective factors into cognitive theories can be traced at least back to Schacter and Singer's (1962) work; however, the leading theorist in this area now appears to be Mandler (1975, 1984).

Mandler's general theory is presented in some detail in his 1984 book, and he has recently described his view of how the theory can be applied to the teaching and learning of mathematical problem solving (Mandler, 1989). At the risk of oversimplification, only a brief summary of his theory will be presented here.

Mandler's view is that most affective factors arise out of the emotional responses to the interruption of plans or planned behavior. In Mandler's terms, plans arise from the activation of a schema. The schema produces an action sequence, and if the anticipated sequence of actions cannot be completed, the blockage or discrepancy is followed by a physiological response. This physiological arousal is typically felt as an increase in heartbeat or in muscle tension. The arousal serves as the mechanism for redirecting the individual's attention, and has obvious survival value which presumably may have had some role to play in evolutionary development. At the same time the arousal occurs, the individual attempts to evaluate the meaning of this unexpected or otherwise troublesome blockage. The evaluation of the interruption might classify it in one of several ways: a pleasant surprise, an unpleasant irritation, or perhaps a major catastrophe. The cognitive evaluation of the interruption provides the meaning to the arousal.

There are several important parts to the analysis of the meaning of the interruptions. First, the meaning comes out of the cognitive interpretation of the arousal. This meaning will be dependent on what the individual knows or assumes to be true. In other words, the individual's knowledge and beliefs play a significant role in the interpretation of the interruption. The role of the culture that shapes the beliefs would seem to be particularly important.

Second, the arousal that leads to the emotion is generally of limited duration. Normal individuals adjust to the unexpected event, interpret it in the context in which it occurs, and try to find some other way to carry out their plan and achieve their goal. The emotion may be intense, but it is generally transitory in normal individuals, at least initially.

Third, repeated interruptions in the same context will result in emotions that become less intense. The individual will reduce the demand on cognitive processing by responding more and more automatically, and with less and less intensity. The responses in this situation become more stable and predictable, and begin to resemble the kinds of attitudes that have been the emphasis of past research on affect in mathematics education.

To help clarify the situation, consider the affective responses of a sixth-grade student to a typical story problem. Suppose that the student believes that story problems should make sense and should have a reasonable answer that can be obtained in a minute or two. Suppose also that the student has had some success in other areas of mathematics. If the student is unable to obtain a satisfactory answer in a reasonable time, the failure to solve the problem (an interruption of the plan) is likely to lead to some arousal. The interpretation of this arousal is likely to be negative, and is often reported as frustration by students who are able to verbalize their feelings. If the students are able to overcome the blockage and find a solution to the problem, they may report positive reactions to the experience. If negative reactions to story problems occur repeatedly, the response to story problems will eventually become automatic and stable. In this situation the student would have developed a negative attitude toward story problems.

In summary, there appear to be at least three major facets of the affective experience of mathematics students that are worthy of further study. First, students hold certain beliefs about mathematics and about themselves that play an important role in the development of their affective responses to mathematical situations. Second, since interruptions and blockages are an inevitable part of the learning of mathematics, the students will experience both positive and negative emotions as they learn mathematics; these emotions are likely to be more noticeable when the tasks are novel. Third, the students will develop positive or negative attitudes toward mathematics (or parts of the mathematics curriculum) as they encounter certain mathematical situations repeatedly. These three aspects of affective experience correspond to three areas of research in mathematics education which we will now examine.

BELIEFS, EMOTIONS, AND ATTITUDES IN MATHEMATICS LEARNING

The theoretical analyses of Mandler (1984) and the practical analyses of mathematics classrooms suggest that beliefs, emotions, and attitudes should be important factors in research on the affective domain in mathematics education. A review of some of the relevant literature provides support for the importance of these three constructs.

Beliefs

There seem to be two major categories of beliefs that have an influence on mathematics learners: beliefs about mathematics and beliefs about self. The discussion of these categories will be followed by comments on teachers' beliefs about mathematics and instruction.

Beliefs about mathematics. Research on student beliefs about mathematics has received considerable attention over recent years. The National Assessment of Educational Progress has included items related to beliefs about mathematics for some time. The most recent assessment (Brown et al., 1988) indicates that students believe that mathematics is important, difficult, and based on rules. These beliefs about mathematics, although not emotional in themselves, certainly would tend to generate more intense reactions to mathematical tasks than beliefs that mathematics is unimportant, easy, and based on logical reasoning.

Research on beliefs has been highlighted by the results of research on problem solving. As Schoenfeld (1985) and

Silver (1985) have pointed out, student beliefs about mathematics may weaken their ability to solve nonroutine problems. If students believe that mathematical problems should always be completed in five minutes or less, they may be unwilling to persist in trying to solve problems that may take substantially longer for most students. Nevertheless, this kind of belief has been generated out of the typical classroom context in which students see mathematics. There is nothing wrong with the students' mechanism for developing beliefs about mathematics; what needs to be changed is the curriculum (and beyond that, the culture) that generates such beliefs.

Another important area of research on beliefs comes mainly out of the work on gender differences in mathematics education. Most of the data have come from studies that used the Fennema and Sherman (1976) scales, especially the scale on the perceived usefulness of mathematics. Fennema (1989), in summarizing this research, notes that males in general report higher perceived usefulness than females. Other scales (for example, mathematics as a male domain) also deal with beliefs about mathematics. These kinds of beliefs are important both for gender differences in mathematics achievement and for the related differences between females and males in affective responses to mathematics.

Beliefs about self. Research on self-concept, confidence, and causal attributions related to mathematics tends to focus on beliefs about the self. These beliefs about self are closely related to notions of metacognition and self-awareness. Again, in mathematics education the research on gender differences has taken the lead in this area.

Research on self-concept and confidence in learning mathematics indicates that there are substantial differences between males and females on this dimension. Reyes (1984) and Meyer and Fennema (1988) summarized the relevant literature. In general, males tend to be more confident than females, even when females may have better reasons based on their performance to feel confident. The influence of confidence on mathematical performance, especially in the area of nonroutine problem solving, seems relatively direct.

Another set of beliefs about self has been investigated quite thoroughly under the rubric of causal attributions of success and failure. Although there are several antecedents of this work and many different applications of the ideas, the central themes are well explicated in a recent reformulation of the theory by Weiner (1986). The three main dimensions of the theory deal with the locus (internal or external), the stability (for example, ability vs. effort), and the controllability of the causal agent. For example, a student who fails to solve a mathematics problem could say that the problem was too hard—a cause that is external, stable, and uncontrollable by the student. A student who succeeds in solving a problem might attribute that success to effort—a cause that is internal, unstable, and controllable.

The nature of the attributions of female and male students has been important in recent research in mathematics education, and the studies have provided some of the most consistent results in the literature on the affective domain. For example, males are more likely than females to attribute their success in mathematics to ability, and females are more likely than males to attribute their failures to lack of ability. In addition, females tend to attribute their successes to extra effort more than males do, and males tend to attribute their failures to lack of effort more than females do. The resulting differences in participation in mathematically related careers appear to reflect these gender differences in attributions (Fennema, 1989; Fennema & Peterson, 1985; Meyer & Fennema, 1988; Reyes, 1984).

Teachers' beliefs. So far our discussion has concentrated on students' beliefs about mathematics and about themselves. But there is a corresponding set of beliefs that teachers hold about mathematics, mathematics teaching, and themselves that are also important to the study of affect in mathematics education. There have been a number of important studies of teachers' beliefs about mathematics (for example, Thompson, 1984), and current recommendations for a research agenda on mathematics teaching suggest that more work be done in this area (Cooney, Grouws, & Jones, 1988). There are also studies of teachers' beliefs about instruction (Peterson & Barger, 1985), as well as research on teachers' attributions (Prawat, Byers, & Anderson, 1983); these investigations are more directly related to affective factors in classroom instruction. However, most of the research along these lines does not deal specifically with mathematics teaching.

In summary, research on beliefs and their influence on students and teachers has been an important theme in investigations of learning and instruction in mathematics. Some of this research is directly connected with affective issues (for example, confidence), but much of it is not. Since beliefs provide an important part of the context within which emotional responses to mathematics develop, we need to establish stronger connections between research on beliefs and research on emotions in the context of mathematics classrooms.

Emotions

The emotional reactions of students have not been major factors in research on affect in mathematics education. This lack of attention to emotion is probably due, in part, to the fact that research on affective issues has generally looked for factors that are stable and can be measured by questionnaire. To phrase this observation in another way, most research from the past has looked at products, not at processes. However, there have been a number of studies that have looked at the processes involved in learning mathematics, and these studies have sometimes paid attention to the emotions. In this section, we review briefly a few of these studies.

One of the early studies of problem-solving processes was conducted by Bloom and Broder (1950). In this work they noted how students' engagement in the task led them into periods of tension and frustration, especially when they felt that their attempts to reach a solution were blocked. Once the block had been overcome, the students would relax and report very positive emotions. This study was conducted before the current focus on cognition became common, and it is justifiably recognized as an early exemplar of research on cognitive processes. It also provides a useful model for integrating research on cognition and affect.

Reports of strong emotional reactions to mathematics do not appear in the research literature very often. An important exception is the work of Buxton (1981). His research deals with adults who report their emotional reaction to mathematical tasks as panic. Their reports of panic are accompanied by a high degree of physiological arousal; this arousal is so difficult to control that they find it disrupts their ability to concentrate on the task. Their emotional reactions are also described as fear, anxiety, and embarrassment. Buxton interpreted these data in terms of Skemp's (1979) views of the affective domain, and suggested a number of strategies to change students' beliefs in order to reduce the intensity of the emotional response.

A number of other researchers have investigated factors that are related to the influence of emotions on cognitive processes in mathematics. Wagner, Rachlin, and Jensen (1984) reported that algebra students who were stuck on a problem would sometimes get upset and grope wildly for any response, no matter how irrational, that would get them past the blockage. On a more positive note, Brown and Walter (1983) found that making conjectures can be a source of great joy to mathematics students. In a similar way, Mason, Burton, and Stacey (1982) talked about the satisfaction of the "Aha!" experience in mathematical problem solving, and made suggestions for encouraging students to savor and anticipate that positive emotional experience. Lawler (1981) also documented the positive emotional responses that accompany that moment of insight when a child first sees the connections between two important ideas.

Although comments about emotion do appear in the research literature from time to time, it is fairly unusual for research on mathematics education to include measures of physiological changes that accompany the emotions. An exception is a recent study by Gentry and Underhill (1987) in which they used physical measurements of muscle tension as well as paper-and-pencil measures of anxiety toward mathematics. As one might expect, there was little correlation between the two measures, suggesting that traditional measures of anxiety may be quite different from the emotional responses that influence students in the classroom.

In summary, research on emotional responses to mathematics has been with us for some time, but it has never played a prominent part in research on the affective domain in mathematics. A major problem has been the lack of a theoretical framework within which to interpret the role of the emotions in the learning of mathematics. Mandler's (1984) theory should help to provide such a framework. Meanwhile, the available data from a variety of sources and a variety of theoretical perspectives suggest that careful observation of students, along with detailed interviews, should allow researchers to make sense of the emotional states of mathematics learners (McLeod, 1988).

Attitudes

Research on attitudes towards mathematics has a relatively long history. For recent reviews and analyses, see Haladyna, Shaughnessy, and Shaughnessy (1983), Kulm (1980), Leder (1987), and Reyes (1984). In this paper the term *attitude* is reserved for affective responses that involve positive or negative feelings of moderate intensity and reasonable stability. Examples of attitudes toward mathematics would include liking geometry, disliking story problems, being curious about topology, and being bored by algebra. As Leder (1987) and others have noted, attitudes toward mathematics are not a unidimensional factor; there are many different kinds of mathematics, as well a variety of different feelings about each type of mathematics.

Attitudes toward mathematics appear to develop in two different ways. One was referred to earlier: attitudes may result from the automatizing of a repeated emotional reaction to mathematics. For example, if a student has repeated negative experiences with geometric proofs, the emotional impact will usually lessen in intensity over time. Eventually the emotional reaction to geometric proof will become more automatic, there will be less physiological arousal, and the response will become a stable one that can probably be measured through use of a questionnaire. A second source of attitudes is the assignment of an already existing attitude to a new but related task. A student who has a negative attitude toward geometric proof may attach that same attitude to proofs in algebra. To phrase this process in cognitive terminology, the attitude from one schema is attached to a second related schema. For a more detailed discussion of a cognitive approach to the formation of attitudes, see Abelson (1976) and Marshall (1989).

If we think of attitudes as the end result of emotional reactions that have become automatized, then we can predict that there could be an attitude that corresponds to every emotion. Students who are fearful in certain mathematical settings can eventually become chronically anxious. If a student regularly has positive experiences with nonroutine mathematical problems, an attitude of curiosity about problem solving could develop.

CURRENT RESEARCH LINKING COGNITION AND AFFECT

Given the importance of affective factors to learning and instruction in mathematics, it seems reasonable to try to devise theories that can link the cognitive and affective domains. In this paper Mandler's (1984) theoretical position has received considerable attention, but he is not the only person who has tried to build a theory that connects cognition and affect. For example, Beck and Emery (1985), Dweck (1986), and Meichenbaum (1977) have all written on this general topic. However, Mandler has probably been the most explicit in terms of trying to connect cognitive science, affect, and mathematics learning at the same time

(Mandler, 1989). In the next section we consider a number of studies that explore these connections between cognition, affect, and mathematics education.

The studies will be discussed under the categories of learning and teaching to indicate the focus of the research. The methodology in each case is familiar to readers of the cognitive literature. There is heavy emphasis on verbal protocols and occasional comparisons of experts to novices. Many of these studies were completed in connection with a grant from the National Science Foundation (McLeod & Adams, 1989).

Studies of Learning

Research on learning with young children often provides opportunities to include affect, particularly in studies that are designed to investigate cognitive issues. For example, Marshall (1989) reports on the affective reactions of sixth-grade students to mathematical story problems. Although the main purpose of the research was to investigate children's development of schemas for story problems, the interviewer also encouraged students to verbalize their affective reactions to the problems. Given this opportunity to discuss their feelings in a supportive environment, many children responded quite freely. Some of the children had rather intense emotional reactions, including a few who discovered something new about mathematics during the solution of the problems and who were delighted with their new knowledge. A few others demonstrated negative reactions to the problems, including one child who reported a rapid heartbeat as well as general discomfort and fear during the interview. In this case the interviewer ended the questions and spent some time reassuring the child. The source of this child's difficulty appeared to be the blockage that the child experienced in attempting to solve a nonroutine problem. Most children, however, used their verbal comments to express well-established attitudes about story problems; these attitudes often revealed negative views toward mathematics or toward themselves as problem solvers. In Marshall's analysis, these emotional and attitudinal responses were attached to various components of the schemas involved in solving story problems.

Marshall's procedures and analysis provide a good example of how simply a study with cognitive objectives can be expanded to include affective issues in a natural way. In another study involving story problems, L. Sowder (1989) was also able to detect the influence of affective responses to the problems. In his study he found more intense affective responses to story problems that involved multiplying or dividing by decimals less than one. Since multiplication or division by numbers less than one contradicts some students' expectation that "multiplication makes bigger, division makes smaller," the more intense affective responses presumably reflect those students' reaction to this discrepancy, as Mandler's theory would predict.

In a third study involving story problems, this time at the seventh-grade level, Lester, Garofalo, and Kroll (1989) focused mainly on the role of metacognition in problem solving. In order to explain the context in which these metacognitive decisions were made, the researchers also gathered data on affective factors, including children's beliefs about themselves as problem solvers and their attitudes toward mathematical problem solving. The data from this study support the view that the social context and the beliefs which it engenders have an important influence on both the students' affective responses as well as their metacognitive acts.

An increasingly important part of the context for problem solving is the use of computers as tools for instruction. Kaput (1989) discussed the implication of computers for students' affective reactions to instruction. He observed that computer environments for teaching algebra or geometry change not only the social context of instruction, but also the opportunities for students to discover their own errors. No longer need an outsider (like a teacher or peer) be seen as an authority who corrects errors; now the technology can provide students with ways of determining for themselved what needs to be corrected. Kaput's analysis should help stimulate the development of innovative software that pays more attention to the role of affect in a technological environment.

These studies of children's learning indicate that affect plays an important role in the performance of novice problem solvers. Silver and Metzger (1989) provided related data on the performance of experts. In their study, Silver and Metzger interviewed research mathematicians and asked them to solve nonroutine problems while thinking aloud. These interviews provide a rich source of data on the relationship between the affective domain and expertise in mathematical problem solving. A striking result from these data is the important role played by aesthetics in the monitoring and evaluation of expert performance. Rather than viewing problems from a utilitarian perspective, these experts spoke frequently about the elegance, harmony, and coherence of various solutions (or attempted solutions) to problems. The aesthetic aspects of the problem-solving experience were clearly linked to the experts' emotional responses, including their enjoyment of the problem.

Although the studies cited above were stimulated by Mandler's ideas, other research with a cognitive orientation has been including affective factors for some time. For example, Peterson (1988) summarized a series of studies that have included lengthy interviews with students who were asked to comment on affective as well as cognitive matters. There is also some work on the development of early number concepts that gives affect serious consideration; Ginsburg and Allardice (1984) provided an intriguing view of how beliefs and emotion can contribute to the difficulties of young children who are unsuccessful in mathematics. These and other studies suggest that the usual methods for research on cognition can be adapted to include proper attention to the role of affect (including its more intense, emotional forms) in the learning of mathematics.

Studies of Teaching

Research on teachers and teaching in mathematics education seldom focuses on the affective factors that are frequently so visible in classrooms. This section will discuss several papers that do include affect, and do so in ways that go beyond the traditional attitude measures.

Cobb, Yackel, and Wood (1989) have provided extensive data on how a teacher in a second-grade classroom dealt with emotions in the learning of mathematics. The data were obtained through careful observation of the classroom over an entire school year. The observers were able to document how the teacher worked with the students as they developed beliefs about mathematics. For example, the teacher was very explicit about the need to justify answers to mathematical problems, and about the importance of the justification. She was also explicit in her specifications of the acceptable kinds of behavior regarding solving mathematical problems. For example, she repeatedly emphasized the satisfactions that come with solving problems independently, and instructed students not to tell the answers to those who were still working on the problems. She was very clear in letting the students know that persistence, in spite of frustration, was important to success in solving problems. Since this classroom's expectations differed from what had been expected of the students in other contexts, the changed norms were explicitly taught and practiced, and the teacher worked hard to see that they were adhered to. The result was a classroom where students showed a lot of satisfaction and enthusiasm for problem solving, and demonstrated an autonomous view of themselves as learners.

In a study of preservice teachers' estimation skills, J. Sowder (1989) investigated the teachers' tolerance for error, their attributions of success and failure, and other beliefs about mathematics and about themselves. Through extensive interviews with a sample of teachers, Sowder was able to create a profile of the beliefs that characterized good and poor estimators. Good estimators tended to have strong self-concepts with regard to mathematics, to attribute successes to their ability rather than just to effort, and to hold the belief that estimation was important. Poor estimators were more likely to have a weak self-concept in mathemat-

ics, to attribute successes to effort, and not to value estimation. The exceptions to these general patterns were interesting cases that showed how individual beliefs about
mathematics could have an important impact on individual
performance on estimation tasks. The general conclusions
of this study provide some indication of the difficulties that
will be involved in implementing recommendations to include estimation in the elementary mathematics curriculum. Clearly many teachers who are in the field, as well as
many more who are on their way, do not hold beliefs about
mathematics or about themselves that are compatible with
the goals of the curriculum in terms of estimation skills (J.
Sowder, 1989).

In a third study of teachers, Grouws and Cramer (1989)
observed six expert teachers of problem solving at the junior
high school level. The focus of this study was on identifying
the affective characteristics of the classrooms of these
teachers during problem-solving lessons. Each teacher was
observed five to seven times over the course of the semester.
The observations revealed that students enjoyed problem
solving, persevered on problem-solving tasks, and worked
willingly on problem-solving assignments. Interviews with
teachers helped with the identification of strategies that led
to this positive affective climate in the classroom. For example, teachers appeared to work hard to establish a good
relationship with students. They tended to be friendly
rather than formal, and to share personal anecdotes about
their own problem solving that illustrated their own
strengths and weaknesses as problem solvers. In addition,
the teachers established a system that held students accountable for their performance in problem solving. The
system itself varied, although most teachers did pay attention to more than just the answer to the problem. Also, the
teachers made frequent use of cooperative groups, and
noted that small-group work tended to promote indepen-
dence and reduce feelings of frustration. Although no single factor appeared to be the cause of the success of these
expert teachers, further research should provide indica-
tions of how these classroom characteristics contribute to

the development of positive affective environments for problem solving.

These studies of teachers and teaching provide useful information on how beliefs, emotions, and attitudes play a significant role in mathematics instruction. There are, of course, other researchers who are considering affective factors in some detail as well. Tittle (1987), for example, has provided teachers with data on students' affective characteristics, thus making it possible for teachers to tailor instruction for students' affective as well as cognitive characteristics. This approach could be particularly important for gender differences in mathematics education (Tittle, 1986). Finally, Brophy (1986) has been concerned with improving the motivational climate in classrooms through strategies for encouraging enthusiasm for learning, reducing anxiety, and inducing curiosity. Further research on affect in classrooms should provide more guidance on these topics.

MODELS FOR RESEARCH AND
CURRICULUM DEVELOPMENT

In a recent paper, Carpenter and Fennema (1988) proposed a model for integrating cognitive and instructional science that would guide research and curriculum development in mathematics. The model includes three main categories and their interrelationships. The three categories include teachers' knowledge, beliefs, and decisions; classroom instruction; and students' cognitions, behaviors, and learning. Although affect is implied by some parts of this model (for example, the emphasis on teacher beliefs) the model would be strengthened if the role of affect in learning were made more explicit.

The incorporation of affect in the model could be accomplished in a number of different ways. For example, the box that lists student cognition could be expanded to include affect as well as cognition. Alternatively, the affective domain could be added as a separate box that is connected to all the others, encouraging us to think about affect as an

additional dimension of the model that has an influence on
all the other parts. But this expansion of the model, although helpful, would not address an underlying concern.
This model, like many in cognitive science, allows the
reader to assume that affective issues can be separated
from cognitive processes, that the two domains are dis-
crete in some fundamental sense. In contrast, Mandler
(1989) argued that affective responses are not separate
processors labeled fear or joy; instead, affective responses
are generated from the cognitive evaluations of individual
responses to various events in people's lives, especially the
unexpected events. Students' affective responses to these
discrepant events lead them to establish response patterns
to the various routine or novel situations that they face
every day.

Moreover, affect is not merely a characteristic of students; it is also a characteristic of teachers. At the moment,
teachers' abilities to deal with affective issues in the classroom are not an important focus of instruction in teacher
preparation programs. These abilities are probably taken
into account in some informal and largely tacit way during
selection and evaluation procedures, but teacher education
programs do not appear to make a serious effort to develop
teachers' understanding of their own or their students' affective responses to mathematics. A revised version of Carpenter and Fennema's (1988) model could provide an exemplar of how to incorporate affect and cognition in a
framework that would guide both teacher education and research.

The model also needs to encourage researchers to think
about affect as a part of human activity that is accessible to
researchers through typical cognitive methods. Too often
cognitive researchers are not willing to apply to questions
related to affect the same qualitative research methods that
they use in their cognitive investigations. When researchers limit themselves to quantitative analyses of data that
are gathered by questionnaire, they limit themselves to
only a part of the affective domain (typically beliefs and attitudes), and neglect the more emotional aspects of student

learning. The neglect of emotion in research on cognition means that the basis for the development of attitudes (and to some extent, beliefs) is neglected as well. Moreover, the emotions may be the most relevant part of the affective domain to the study of cognitive processes. For example, if an interruption or discrepant event causes an emotional reaction that uses up a student's limited short-term memory for the cognitive evaluation of the event, there will be less mental capacity available for problem solving.

In conclusion, research on the affective domain suggests that affect plays a central role in learning and instruction in mathematics. Affective factors should be incorporated in more cognitively guided research studies; frequently, the additional data on affective factors could be gathered with little additional effort. However, researchers would need to become familiar with current conceptions of affective issues, and identify theoretical frameworks that were compatible with their own research questions.

REFERENCES

Abelson, R. P. (1976). Script processing in attitude formation and decision making. In J. S. Carroll & J. W. Payne (Eds.), *Cognition and social behavior* (pp. 33 – 45). Hillsdale, NJ: Lawrence Erlbaum Associates.

Azjen, I., & Fishbein, M. (1980). *Understanding attitudes and predicting social behavior.* Englewood Cliffs, NJ: Prentice-Hall.

Bearison, D. J., & Zimilies, N. (1986). *Thought and emotion: Developmental perspectives.* Hillsdale, NJ: Lawrence Erlbaum Associates.

Beck, A. T., & Emery, G. (1985). *Anxiety disorders and phobias: A cognitive perspective.* New York: Basic Books.

Bloom, B. S., & Broder, L. J. (1950). *Problem-solving processes of college students.* Chicago: University of Chicago Press.

Brophy, J. (1986). *On motivating students.* Unpublished manuscript, Michigan State University, Institute for Research on Teaching, East Lansing.

Brown, C. A., Carpenter, T. P., Kouba, V. L., Lindquist, M. M., Silver, E. A., & Swafford, J. O. (1988). Secondary school results for the Fourth NAEP Mathematics Assessment: Algebra, geometry, mathematical methods, and attitudes. *The Mathematics Teacher, 81,* 337–347, 397.

Brown, S. I., & Walter, M. (1983). *The art of problem posing.* Philadelphia: Franklin Institute Press.

Buxton, L. (1981). *Do you panic about maths?: Coping with maths anxiety.* London: Heinemann.

Carpenter, T. P., & Fennema, E. (1988). *Research and cognitively guided instruction.* Madison, WI: National Center for Research in Mathematical Sciences Education.

Cobb, P. (1985). Two children's anticipations, beliefs, and motivations. *Educational Studies in Mathematics, 16,* 111–126.

Cobb, P., Yackel, E., & Wood, T. (1989). Young children's emotional acts while engaging in mathematical problem solving. In D. B. McLeod & V. M. Adams (Eds.), *Affect and mathematical problem solving: A new perspective* (pp. 117–148). New York: Springer-Verlag.

Commission on Standards for School Mathematics. (1989). *Curriculum and evaluation standards for school mathematics.* Reston, VA: National Council of Teachers of Mathematics.

Cooney, T. J., Grouws, D. A., & Jones, D. (1988). An agenda for research on teaching mathematics. In D. A. Grouws, T. J. Cooney, & D. Jones (Eds.), *Research agenda for mathematics education: Effective mathematics teaching* (pp. 253–261). Reston, VA: National Council of Teachers of Mathematics.

Dweck, C. S. (1986). Motivational processes affecting learning. *American Psychologist, 41,* 1040–1048.

Fennema, E. (1989). The study of affect and mathematics: A proposed generic model for research. In D. B. McLeod & V. M. Adams (Eds.), *Affect and mathematical problem solving: A new perspective* (pp. 205–219). New York: Springer-Verlag.

Fennema, E., & Peterson, P. (1985). Autonomous learning behavior: A possible explanation of gender-related differences in mathematics. In L. C. Wilkinson & C. Marrett (Eds.), *Gender influences in classroom interaction* (pp. 17–35). Orlando, FL: Academic Press.

Fennema, E., & Sherman, J. A. (1976). Fennema-Sherman Mathematics Attitude Scales: Instruments designed to measure attitudes toward the learning of mathematics by females and males. *Journal for Research in Mathematics Education, 7,* 324–326.

Frieze, I. H. (1976). The role of information processing in making causal attributions for success and failure. In J. S. Carroll & J. W. Payne (Eds.), *Cognition and social behavior* (pp. 95–112).

Hillsdale, NJ: Lawrence Erlbaum Associates.

Gardner, H. (1985). *The mind's new science.* New York: Basic Books.

Gentry, W. M., & Underhill, R. (1987). A comparison of two palliative methods of intervention for the treatment of mathematics anxiety among female college students. *Proceedings of the Eleventh International Conference on the Psychology of Mathematics Education, 11,* 99–105.

Ginsburg, H. P., & Allardice, B. S. (1984). Children's difficulties with school mathematics. In B. Rogoff & J. Lave (Eds.), *Everyday cognition: Its development in social context* (pp. 194–219). Cambridge: Harvard University Press.

Grouws, D. A., & Cramer, K. (1989). Teaching practices and student affect in problem solving lessons of select junior high mathematics teachers. In D. B. McLeod & V. M. Adams (Eds.), *Affect and mathematical problem solving: A new perspective* (pp. 149–161). New York: Springer-Verlag.

Haladyna, T., Shaughnessy, J., & Shaughnessy, J. M. (1983). A causal analysis of attitude toward mathematics. *Journal for Research in Mathematics Education, 14,* 19–29.

Hart, L. E. (1989). Describing the affective domain: Saying what we mean. In D. B. McLeod & V. M. Adams (Eds.), *Affect and mathematical problem solving: A new perspective* (pp. 37–48). New York: Springer-Verlag.

Kagan, J. (1978). On emotion and its development: A working paper. In M. Lewis & L. A. Rosenblum (Eds.), *The development of affect* (pp. 11–41). New York: Plenum Press.

Kaput, J. J. (1989). Information technologies and affect in mathematical experiences. In D. B. McLeod & V. M. Adams (Eds.), *Affect and mathematical problem solving: A new perspective* (pp. 89–103). New York: Springer-Verlag.

Kloosterman, P. (1988). Self-confidence and motivation in mathematics. *Journal of Educational Psychology, 80,* 345–351.

Kulm, G. (1980). Research on mathematics attitude. In R. J. Shumway (Ed.), *Research in mathematics education* (pp. 356–387). Reston, VA: National Council of Teachers of Mathematics.

Lawler, R. W. (1981). The progressive construction of mind. *Cognitive Science, 5,* 1–30.

Leder, G. C. (1987). Attitudes towards mathematics. In T. A. Romberg & D. M. Stewart (Eds.), *The monitoring of school mathematics* (pp. 261–277). Madison: Wisconsin Center for Education Research.

Lester, F. K., Garofalo, J., & Kroll, D. L. (1989). Self-confidence, interest, beliefs, and metacognition: Key influences on problem-solving behavior. In D. B. McLeod & V. M. Adams (Eds.), *Affect and mathematical problem solving: A new perspective* (pp. 75–88). New York: Springer-Verlag.

Ligault, L. (1987). Investigation des facteurs cognitifs et affectifs dans les blocages en mathématiques. In J. C. Bergeron, N. Herscovics, & C. Kieran (Eds.), *Proceedings of the Eleventh International Conference on the Psychology of Mathematics Education* (Vol. 1, pp. 120–125). Montreal: University of Montreal.

Mandler, G. (1972). Helplessness: Theory and research in anxiety. In C. D. Spielberger (Ed.), *Anxiety: Current trends in theory and research* (pp. 359–374). New York: Academic Press.

———. (1975). *Mind and emotion.* New York: Wiley.

———. (1984). *Mind and body: Psychology of emotion and stress.* New York: Norton.

———. (1985). *Cognitive psychology: An essay in cognitive science.* Hillsdale, NJ: Lawrence Erlbaum Associates.

———. (1989). *Affect and learning: Causes and consequences of emotional interactions.* In D. B. McLeod & V. M. Adams (Eds.), *Affect and mathematical problem solving: A new perspective* (pp. 3–19). New York: Springer-Verlag.

Marshall, S. (1989). Affect in schema knowledge: Source and impact. In D. B. McLeod and V. M. Adams (Eds.), *Affect and mathematical problem solving: A new perspective* (pp. 49–58). New York: Springer-Verlag.

Mason, J., Burton, L., & Stacey, K. (1982). *Thinking mathematically.* London: Addison-Wesley.

McLeod, D. B. (1988). Affective issues in mathematical problem solving: Some theoretical considerations. *Journal for Research in Mathematics Education, 19,* 134–141.

McLeod, D. B., & Adams, V. M. (Eds.). (1989). *Affect and mathematical problem solving: A new perspective.* New York: Springer-Verlag.

Meichenbaum, D. (1977). *Cognitive behavior modification: An integrative approach.* New York: Plenum Press.

Meyer, M. R., & Fennema, E. (1988). Girls, boys, and mathematics. In T. R. Post (Ed.), *Teaching mathematics in grades K–8: Research-based methods* (pp. 406–425). Boston: Allyn and Bacon.

Nimier, J. (1977). Mathematique et affectivity. *Educational Studies in Mathematics, 8,* 241–250.

Norman, D. A. (1981). Twelve issues for cognitive science. In D.

A. Norman (Ed.), *Perspectives on cognitive science* (pp. 265 – 295). Norwood, NJ: Ablex.

Peterson, P. L. (1988). Teaching for higher-order thinking in mathematics: The challenge for the next decade. In D. A. Grouws & T. J. Cooney (Eds.), *Research agenda for mathematics education: Effective mathematics teaching* (pp. 2 – 26). Reston, VA: National Council of Teachers of Mathematics.

Peterson, P. L., & Barger, S. A. (1985). Attribution theory and teacher expectancy. In J. B. Dusek (Ed.), *Teacher expectancies* (pp. 159 – 184). Hillsdale, NJ: Lawrence Erlbaum Associates.

Piaget, J. (1981). *Intelligence and affectivity: Their relationship during child development.* Palo Alto, CA: Annual Reviews.

Prawat, R. S., Byers, J. L., & Anderson, A. H. (1983). An attributional analysis of teachers' affective reactions to student success and failure. *American Educational Research Journal, 20,* 137 – 152.

Reyes, L. H. (1984). Affective variables and mathematics education. *Elementary School Journal, 84,* 558 – 581.

Schacter, S., & Singer, J. (1962). Cognitive, social and physiological determinants of emotional state. *Psychological Review, 69,* 379 – 399.

Schoenfeld, A. H. (1985). *Mathematical problem solving.* Orlando, FL: Academic Press.

————. (1987). Cognitive science and mathematics education: An overview. In A. H. Schoenfeld (Ed.), *Cognitive science and mathematics education* (pp. 1 – 31). Hillsdale, NJ: Lawrence Erlbaum Associates.

Sigel, I. E. (1986). Cognition-affect: A psychological riddle. In D. J. Bearison & N. Zimilies (Eds.), *Thought and emotion: Developmental perspectives* (pp. 211 – 229). Hillsdale, NJ: Lawrence Erlbaum Associates.

Silver, E. A. (1985). Research on teaching mathematical problem solving: Some underrepresented themes and needed directions. In E. A. Silver (Ed.), *Teaching and learning mathematical problem solving: Multiple research perspectives* (pp. 247 – 266). Hillsdale, NJ: Lawrence Erlbaum Associates.

Silver, E. A., & Metzger, W. R. (1989). Aesthetic influences on expert mathematical problem solving. In D. B. McLeod & V. M. Adams (Eds.), *Affect and mathematical problem solving: A new perspective* (pp. 59 – 74). New York: Springer-Verlag.

Simon, H. A. (1967). Motivational and emotional controls of cognition. *Psychological Review, 74,* 29 – 39.

————. (1982). Comments. In M. S. Clark & S. T. Fiske (Eds.), *Affect and cognition* (pp. 333–342). Hillsdale, NJ: Lawrence Erlbaum Associates.

Skemp, R. R. (1979). *Intelligence, learning, and action.* New York: Wiley.

Skinner, B. F. (1953). *Science and human behavior.* New York: Macmillan.

Snow, R. E., & Farr, M. J. (1987). *Aptitude, learning, and instruction: Volume 3: Conative and affective process analyses.* Hillsdale, NJ: Lawrence Erlbaum Associates.

Sowder, J. T. (1989). Affective factors and computational estimation ability. In D. B. McLeod & V. M. Adams (Eds.), *Affect and mathematical problem solving: A new perspective* (pp. 177–191). New York: Springer-Verlag.

Sowder, L. (1989). Searching for affect in the solution of story problems in mathematics. In D. B. McLeod & V. M. Adams (Eds.), *Affect and mathematical problem solving: A new perspective* (pp. 104–113). New York: Springer-Verlag.

Thompson, A. G. (1984). The relationship of teachers' conceptions of mathematics and mathematics teaching to instructional practice. *Educational Studies in Mathematics, 15,* 105–127.

Tittle, C. K. (1986). Gender research and education. *American Psychologist, 41,* 1161–1168.

————. (1987). *A project to improve mathematics instruction for women and minorities: Comprehensive assessment and mathematics.* Unpublished manuscript, City University of New York, Graduate School and University Center, New York.

von Glasersfeld, E. (1987). Learning as a constructive activity. In C. Janvier (Ed.), *Problems of representation in the teaching and learning of mathematics* (pp. 3–17). Hillsdale, NJ: Lawrence Erlbaum Associates.

Wagner, S., Rachlin, S. L., & Jensen, R. J. (1984). *Algebra learning project: Final Report.* Athens: University of Georgia, Department of Mathematics Education.

Weiner, B. (1982). The emotional consequences of causal attributions. In M. S. Clark & S. T. Fiske (Eds.), *Affect and cognition* (pp. 185–209). Hillsdale, NJ: Lawrence Erlbaum Associates.

————. (1986). *An attributional theory of motivation and emotion.* New York: Springer-Verlag.

4

Curriculum and Teacher Development: Psychological and Anthropological Perspectives*

Paul Cobb, Erna Yackel, and Terry Wood

Like several other research groups, we are currently engaged in a research and development project that addresses the problem of developing a coherent framework within which to talk about both teaching and learning. Given the ongoing nature of our work, much of what follows is speculative and is offered in this spirit. Thus far, several case studies and one quantitative analysis have been completed. In other aspects of the project, we are still operating as reflective practitioners and are learning by coping with the problems we encounter while working with children and their teachers.

At the pragmatic level, we have drawn on current models of children's early number learning to develop instructional activities for the entire second-grade year. Twenty-four teachers are currently implementing these instructional activities in their classrooms. At a more theoretical level, we are attempting to develop a framework that makes it possible for us to cope with the complexity of classroom life. In

*The project discussed in this paper is supported by the National Science foundation under grants Nos. MDR-847-0400 and MDR 885-0560. All opinions expressed are, of course, solely those of the authors.

doing so, we have had to address basic philosophical issues. We discuss these issues first and then consider the relationship of more specific aspects of the project to the work
of other research groups.

The Paradox of Teaching

The notion that students learn mathematics by actively reorganizing their own experiences is almost universally accepted by the mathematics research community (Resnick,
1983; Romberg & Carpenter, 1986; Steffe, Cobb, & von
Glasersfeld, 1988; von Glasersfeld, 1983). In this view,
mathematical learning is an active problem-solving
process, and what counts as a problem is relative to both
students' current ways of knowing and their intentions or
purposes (Cobb, 1986a; Confrey, 1987; Pask, 1985;
Thompson, 1985). Individuals each construct *their* individual mathematical worlds by reorganizing *their* experiences in an attempt to resolve *their* problems.

   This characterization of mathematical learning is relatively straightforward as long as the focus is solely on individual students. Difficulties arise as soon as students'
learning is considered in the social setting of school instruction. In school, any construction is not as good as any
other — anything does not go. Teachers, in order to fulfill
their wider societal obligations, attempt to realize institutionally sanctioned agendas in their classrooms. They have
in mind things they want students to learn. There is a tension between encouraging students to build on their current understandings on the one hand and initiating students into mathematical culture of the wider community on
the other. As Lampert (1985) put it, the dilemma of teaching "is an argument between opposing tendencies within
oneself in which neither side can come out the winner.
From this perspective, my job [as a mathematics teacher]
would involve maintaining the tension between . . . pushing
students to achieve and providing a comfortable learning
environment, between covering the curriculum and attending to individual understanding" (p. 233). It is the tension
between encouraging students to build on their informal

mathcmatical ways of knowing and attempting to teach them the institutionally sanctioned formal knowledge of codified academic arithmetic that gives rise to the paradox of teaching. Any attempt to help teachers develop forms of classroom practice compatible with constructivism must take seriously the contradictions that teachers have to cope with in the course of their practice. In particular, it must acknowledge that instructional decisions based solely on analyses of students' mathematical knowledge will often be at odds with the institutionally sanctioned goals of instruction.

Decision Making

The term *decision making* is widely used to refer to those moments when teachers consciously think about what they are going to do. As the term has a variety of distinct and, at times, incompatible meanings, we will attempt to clarify our usage.

For researchers interested in computer simulation, it typically denotes the process of achieving a well defined goal by selecting from an array of possible behaviors (Simon, 1976). However, many of the situations that characterize the experience of teaching are paradoxical. There is neither a clearly defined goal nor an array of alternative courses of action (Clark & Lampert, 1986). The teacher has to cope with situations that Schon (1983) called "messes." The teacher might, for example, be torn between two or more incompatible alternatives or simply have difficulty in making sense of the situation. "In three words, teaching is experienced as *complex, uncertain,* and peppered with *dilemmas*" (Clark, 1988, p. 9). For mathematics educators interested in teachers' pedagogical realities, decision making refers to an open-ended problem-solving process. It encompasses problem setting, deliberation, judgment, and questioning the taken-for-granted. Teaching is then more about instigating pedagogical acts of knowing and learning than it is about achieving well-defined instructional goals by choosing from clearly delineated instructional actions. The examples of teachers coping with paradoxes described by

Lampert (1985) give an insight into the creativity that is sometimes involved. In each case, the teacher found a way of coping in a local situation by transcending the interpretation that first gave rise to incompatible alternatives.

This characterization of decision making suggests that teacher education should not be reduced to the specification of lists of behaviors for teachers to perform. Nor is it about programming them to make predetermined decisions (Carpenter & Fennema, 1988). Instead, the emphasis on deliberation and coping implies that

> Research on teaching thinking does not promise to discover a generically effective method or set of techniques for dealing with uncertainty ... [The] teacher educator who abandons the fiction that teaching can become a technically exact enterprise, and who has the courage to reveal how he or she agonizes over real dilemmas and contradictions — that teacher educator is likely to be successful at helping teachers to prepare themselves for uncertainty. (Clark, 1988, p. 10)

Routines

The situations in which teachers consciously deliberate and make decisions about what they are going to do occur against the background of their routine interpretations and actions. The importance of pedagogical routines can be illustrated by drawing on Voigt's (1985) microanalysis of a sequence of twenty-four lessons in which a teacher routinely introduced new mathematics tasks by asking open-ended questions and then directing a whole class discussion with the students. This sounds very nice from the constructivist perspective. A well-intentioned teacher strove to actively involve students in their learning while simultaneously helping the students achieve the goals of instruction. But Voigt's detailed analysis reveals that something else was going on beneath the surface. Unknowingly, the teacher, in fact, funnelled the students towards the solution he had in mind all along by means of implicit markers and nonverbal cues. As a consequence, there was hardly any genuine negotiation of meaning — "the pupils' subjective ideas [were] not explicitly an object of communication" (p. 99). This lack of communication was essential to the success of the teacher's strategy in that the expected solution of a task was attained with the pupils' participation in spite of their lack of competence (p. 96). The teacher fulfilled his obligations to the school as a social institution without falling behind schedule. The illusion of students' active participation in the development of a shared understanding was achieved in the absence of shared understanding. One consequence was that "pupils acquire[d] certain undesirable routines for executing unfamiliar mathematical tasks and [did] not develop a reflective attitude towards the tasks" (p. 111).

Voigt's analysis is, for us, a paradigm case of what can happen as sincere teachers attempt to cope with the paradox inherent in their work. The actions of the teacher observed by Voigt actually undermined the goals he hoped to achieve. This suggests that the task of helping teachers make informed decisions involves, in part, helping them become aware of routinized, taken-for-granted aspects of their practice and encouraging them to consider whether these are compatible with their intentions. We therefore believe that analyses of teachers' thinking should focus on both their conscious decision making and on the routinized, taken-for-granted practices that teachers enact in the two minute intervals between their reports of decisions (Clark & Peterson, 1986). Both focuses provide potential insights into teachers' knowledge and beliefs. For example, the routines that Voigt's teacher enacted reflected the implicit belief that discussions must culminate with apparent agreement on the solution deemed correct. This belief, which is related to the teacher's conception of his role in the institution of the school, can be contrasted with an alternative belief that underlies constructivist teaching and itself becomes taken for granted in practice — namely, that a student's activity is always rational, however bizarre it may at first appear (Labinowicz, 1985; Smedslund, 1977). The trick is to figure out what the student's rationality might be. When this belief becomes taken for granted, the teacher automatically attempts to "get inside students' heads" without first making a conscious decision to do so. And it is against the background of routine interpretations that a situation is framed as one that is anomalous or discrepant and requires a decision (Doyle, 1983; Gadamer, 1986; Hundeide, 1985).

Teachers' Learning

Three speculations concerning the development of teachers' pedagogical content knowledge follow from our emphasis on the dilemmas and paradoxes of teaching and on teachers' implicit classroom routines. First, there is no reason to assume that teachers' pedagogical knowledge consists of a body of decontextualized principles. This leads us to question whether teachers should first be taught general theoretical principles of pedagogical content knowledge and then learn to apply these principles to make practical decisions. A principled model of learning in a particular domain is a formalization of insights gained in the course of many hours of reflective activity. Just as formal mathematics does not capture the way mathematics is constructed and understood (Davis & Hersh, 1981), so principled cognitive models do not capture the way that researchers and teachers initially understand children's mathematics. The formal model is the product of a sequence of abstractions made by the researchers.

We can clarify our argument by drawing an analogy between teachers' construction of pedagogical knowledge and students' construction of mathematical knowledge. As we have seen, the belief that students should be encouraged to use mathematical knowledge constructed in informal settings when they interpret and attempt to solve mathematical tasks encountered in the classroom is a basic tenet of constructivism (Carpenter & Fennema, 1988; Hiebert & Lefevre, 1986; Resnick, 1987; Saxe, 1988). If this is the case in an apparently formal domain such as mathematics, theoretical consistency leads us to argue that it would also be the case with respect to pedagogical knowledge. We know that attempting to directly teach formal mathematics frequently leads to rote learning. Analogously, there is every reason to expect that attempting to transmit formal models to teachers directly will frequently lead to rote teaching. It is the activity that took place in the initial informal phases of modeling that is most relevant to the issue of helping teachers develop their pedagogical knowledge.

Second, we speculate that a case-based approach might be appropriate in helping teachers develop their pedagogical content knowledge. Teachers might share their interpretations of judiciously selected video recordings of students attempting to solve mathematics tasks under the guidance of an expert diagnostician. The example of Voigt's teacher alerts us to the danger of steering the teachers to the interpretation deemed correct by the expert. Rather, the expert's role is to keep the conversation among the teachers going by posing orienting questions before the recording is viewed, framing teachers' conflicting interpretations as issues to be resolved, and bringing to the fore evidence that is in conflict with an interpretation. The immediate goal is that the teachers' increasingly sophisticated interpretations of particular students' mathematical activity might become paradigm cases that they can use to make sense of students' mathematical activity in their classrooms. The wider goal is that they will come to realize that interpretations of students' mathematical activity are eminently discussable and require a rationale.

Our basic point is that teachers' pedagogical content knowledge should build on their informal ways of interpreting and drawing pedagogical implications from students' mathematical activity. The discussion setting is designed to help teachers realize that their current interpretations might be problematic. And the constructivist dictum that knowledge is constructed by reorganizing experience to resolve problems applies as much to teachers (and researchers) as it does to mathematics students. The objective is to help teachers to learn to experience as well as to learn from experience. We should stress that in the absence of empirical data (not to mention models of teachers' construction of pedagogical content knowledge) this remains highly speculative. Nonetheless, it seems more plausible on intuitive grounds than approaches that attempt to teach formal pedagogical knowledge directly. In addition, the social norms the expert attempts to develop in the course of the discussions are compatible with those established by scientific communities (Bernstein, 1983; Brannigan, 1981; Toulmin, 1983).

Finally, the phenomena of implicit routines and dilemmas suggest that teachers should be helped to develop their pedagogical knowledge and beliefs in the context of their classroom practice. It is as teachers interact with their students in concrete situations that they encounter problems that call for reflection and deliberation. These are the occasions where teachers can learn from experience. Discussion of these concrete cases with an observer who suggests an alternative way to frame the situation or simply calls into question some of the teacher's underlying assumptions can guide the teacher's learning. For example, teachers frequently ask us to observe a particular child when we visit their classrooms. In doing so, they voice uncertainties and concerns that have practical significance for them. We can foster their construction of pedagogical content knowledge by helping them develop an interpretation of the child's mathematical activity that leads to a temporary resolution of their difficulty.

It is also in the classroom that teachers' implicit theories, beliefs, and assumptions are expressed in their routine actions. An observer, whether he/she be a researcher or a fellow teacher, can help teachers become aware of and call into question certain aspects of their routine practice that they initially take as self-evident. During our classroom visits, for example, we might ask a teacher how he or she interpreted a particular child's solution attempt. In doing so, we might draw attention to aspects of the child's activity that initially went unnoticed and thus help the teacher make his or her initial routine interpretation problematic.

Our contention that the classroom is a prime setting in

which to facilitate teachers' learning is compatible with the view that theoretical knowledge is derived from, informs, and develops together with pedagogical practice. With regard to our view of the classroom observer's role, we again find ourselves in agreement with Clark (1988) when he stated that the "best consultants are those who leave something interesting and provocative to think about as the clients continue to wrestle with the complexities of the local problematic situation" (p. 6).

Individual Learners and Mathematical Acculturation

The paradox inherent in teaching reflects a basic but deep-rooted epistemological problem. To state the issue bluntly, philosophers who followed Plato's lead and claimed that aspects of the real world are mind-independent have been unable to explain how we can know such a world. Conversely, philosophers who followed the early skeptics and started with aspects of subjective experience have struggled to explain how we experience a shared, objective reality. This poses quite a conundrum for constructivist educators. On the one hand, mathematics education involves acculturating students to a shared mathematical reality. On the other hand, it involves guiding individual students' subjective construction of mathematical knowledge. This, in different form, is the teachers' dilemma of accommodating to individual needs while fulfilling societal obligations. Thus, the paradox of teaching has an epistemological as well as an institutional source.

The most inviting way of coping that we see is to complement psychological constructivism with an anthropological perspective and introduce the notion of community. From this perspective, mathematical knowledge is viewed as the self-evident, taken-for-granted, practical and intellectual activities that have been institutionalized by a community of knowers. For this reason, we prefer to talk of cultural rather than objective mathematical knowledge. This distinction is consistent with the finding that self-evident mathematical practices differ across communities (Carraher & Carraher, 1987; D'Ambrosio, 1985; Lave, 1984;

Saxe, 1988). Further, the cultural perspective captures the evolving nature of mathematical knowledge revealed by historical analysis (Bloor, 1976, 1983; Lakatos, 1976). As cultural knowledge, mathematics is continually regenerated and modified by the coordinated actions of members of a community. We therefore concur with Peirce's (1935) claim that the "very origin of the conception of reality [including mathematical reality] shows that this conception involves the notion of a community" (p. 186).

The suggestion that the psychological perspective should be complimented with an anthropological approach does not resolve the paradox but instead offers a second vantage point from which to view the learning and teaching of mathematics. The psychological and anthropological perspectives constitute nonintersecting domains of description (Bauersfeld, personal communication; Maturana, 1978). When we focus on an individual student's sense-making activity we lose sight of the community, and when we analyze communal knowledge individual sense-making slips from our view. It is not possible to integrate the two perspectives and account for teacher's cognitions, students' cognitions, and the learning-teaching process in an epistemologically sound way within a single, seamless framework. The challenge is to develop ways of coordinating the two perspectives.

As a first step, consider the goals of mathematics education. From the psychological perspective, these are usually stated in terms of helping students to construct increasingly abstract mathematical concepts and procedures. This is the perspective of most mathematics educators. It is assumed "that the development of cognitive skills is central to human development, [and] that these skills appear in regular sequence regardless of context" (Eisenhart, 1988, p. 101). In contrast, the objective from the anthropological perspective is "describing manifestations of the social order in schools and developing frameworks for understanding how students, through exposure to schools, come to learn their place in society" (Eisenhart, 1988, p. 101). This is mathematics education as a process of acculturation rather than of cognitive development. It is here that the notion of mathematics as evolving cultural knowledge rather than as objective, mind-independent knowledge proves crucial for instruction. "Education is (or should be) ... the forum aspect of a culture that gives its participants a role in constantly making and remaking the culture — an active role as participants rather than as performing spectators" (Bruner, 1986, p. 123). It follws that "education, if it is to prepare the young for life as lived, should also partake of the spirit of a forum, of negotiation, of the re-creating of meaning" (p. 123).

From the anthropological perspective, the goal of mathematics education is mathematical acculturation and, Bruner suggests, this should be achieved by nurturing a classroom atmosphere that encourages the negotiation of meaning (Bauersfeld, 1980; Bishop, 1985). Bruner's suggestion is compatible with mathematics educators' concern for individual children's cognitive development, provided we acknowledge that mathematics learning is an interactive as well as constructive activity (Bauersfeld, 1988; Cobb, 1986b, 1989; Cobb, Wood, & Yackel, in press; Confrey, 1987; Steffe, 1987). For example, opportunities for individual children to construct mathematical knowledge arise from attempts to resolve conflicting points of view (Perret-Clermont, 1980), attempts to reconstruct and verbalize a mathematical idea or solution (Levina, 1981), attempts to distance the self from ongoing activity in order to understand an alternative interpretation or solution (Sigel, 1981), and, more generally, from attempts to construct a consensual domain for mathematical activity with others (Barnes & Todd, 1977). In short, "to understand the source and course of cognitive growth, the detailed analysis of social experience is necessary — it is the interaction that is crucial" (Sigel, 1981, p. 216).

By viewing learning as both an interactive and a constructive activity, instructional strategies can be developed that are compatible with general cognitive and anthropological goals. The notion of negotiation emphasizes students' active role in learning. They learn by reorganizing their experiences of interacting with others in an attempt to construct a consensual domain within which to communicate about mathematics. And in doing so, they become acculturated to the mathematical ways of knowing the wider community. Negotiation of meaning implies that each party makes accommodations with respect to the activity of the other. This can be contrasted with the view that changes in students' knowledge are caused by instruction. In the latter view, negotiation and interaction are replaced by a view of the teacher as one who plans instruction to effect students' cognitions on the basis of observations of students' behavior. In this case, students are viewed as cognitive entities to be acted on by teachers in the course of instruction. From our perspective, negotiation and interaction are central to a constructivist view of the learning-teaching process.

Thus far we have attempted to coordinate the goals of instruction from the anthropological and psychological perspectives. A second coordination concerns classroom social life. Most of the time, students act pragmatically and attempt to produce solutions that are acceptable with respect to the classroom situation (Balacheff, 1986). And what counts as acceptable is, of course, relative to the classroom social norms. This suggests that renegotiation of classroom norms profoundly influences students' mathematical activity (Cobb, Yackel, & Wood, 1989; Wood, Cobb, & Yackel, 1990). As we have already noted, social norms should not be equated with formal rules of conduct. Rather, as aspects of the practices of a community, social norms constrain the social activity of individuals whose coordinated activity continually regenerates the social norms. It is in this sense that neither the cognitive nor the anthropological perspectives are primary. For this reason, to focus on one but not the other is to tell half of a good story.

We take students' (and teachers') beliefs to be the cognitive correlates of social norms. (A rationale for this approach can be found in Cobb, Yackel, & Wood, 1989). The three beliefs of interest to us in our current work are beliefs about one's own role, others' roles, and the general nature of mathematical activity. We speculate that a reorganization in any one of these beliefs leads to reorganizations in the other two and that collectively they constitute a belief system. This leads us to propose that students' beliefs are an essential aspect of their cognitions (Cobb, 1985; Confrey, 1984; Schoenfeld, 1985) and should be given as much prominence as teachers' beliefs when instructional issues are considered. In light of Balacheff's observation, we also suggest that social norms be included in analyses of the learning-teaching process (that is, interaction and negotiation).

We have already hinted at a third coordination between the anthropological and psychological perspectives, that concerning mathematical activity. From the psychological perspective, mathematical activity refers to individual students' (or teachers') mathematical ways of knowing. Anthropologically, the teachers and students in a classroom can be viewed as constituting an intellectual community. Mathematical activity then refers to the mathematical practices institutionalized by the members of the community. For example, as we look across video recordings of the second-grade mathematics lessons, we (as observers) see that the practice of operating with units of ten and of one emerges as a taken-for-granted way of doing things. It became taken for granted in that a point was reached after which a child who engaged in this practice was rarely asked to justify this way of doing things. It was beyond justification and emerged as a mathematical truth for the classroom community. It became self-evident to the children that numbers are composed of units of ten and units of one. It became for them a fact about mathematical reality. To be sure, when we interviewed the children individually it became apparent that this practice had a variety of qualitatively distinct meanings for them. Nonetheless, their participation in a classroom community that negotiated and institutionalized certain mathematical practices but not others, profoundly influenced their individual conceptual developments.

More generally, the notion of children's natural mathematics uncontaminated by social context is a fiction. In the classroom we observed intensively, the children constructed their own efficient nonstandard algorithms for adding and subtracting two-digit numbers. These were not natural constructions the children made on their own. They were constrained by the nature of the instructional activities the children completed, the manipulative materials that were made available, and by the requirements that they explain and, when necessary, justify their own interpretations and solutions and attempt to understand the interpretations and solutions of others. In short, they engaged in consensually constrained mathematical activity. Again, neither the psychological nor the anthropological was dominant. The individual children's mathematical activity created the communal mathematical practices that constrained their individual mathematical activity. From the psychological perspective, the children were meaning-makers. From the anthropological perspective, they were truth-makers. As constructivist mathematics educators, we want students to experience intuitions of mind-independent mathematical reality and to experience the discovery of relationships they believe were there all along.

We have argued that the anthropological and psychological perspectives are nonintersecting domains of description. For us, the task is to coordinate rather than integrate analyses of teachers' cognitions, students' cognitions, and social interaction. We have suggested that the classroom social norms and institutionalized mathematical practices be included in analyses of the learning-teaching process and students' beliefs in analyses of their cognitions. We have also introduced the processes of negotiation and institutionalization. This multiperspective approach does not solve the paradox of teaching, but instead suggests coordinations that might prove useful when attempting to cope with it. The multiple perspectives become apparent when we note that experientially meaning is in the world, cognitively it is the learner's head, and anthropologically it is in social interaction.

As a final point, consider the distinction between knowledge and belief. As Peterson, et al. (1987) observed, analyses of teachers' cognitions "raise questions of where 'knowledge' stops and 'beliefs' take over" (p. 53). They further noted that the extent to which beliefs 'can be defended as 'truth' determines the extent to which teachers' 'beliefs' become 'knowledge'" (p. 53). This is an important observation. Knowledge has traditionally been defined as true belief. This, of course, merely leads to the question of what we mean by truth. From the anthropological perspective, knowledge can be defined as institutionalized belief. Truth is then the product of a process of institutionalization. In this regard, research into students' arithmetical word problem solving provides a clear example of the process of institutionalization. The various semantically distinct types of word problems are classified as pedagogical knowledge because they have been negotiated and institutionalized by the mathematics education research community. It is doubtful that these problem types could be considered knowledge without debate even five years ago. Conversely, certain tenets of constructivism are pedagogical beliefs because they have not been institutionalized. In short, the distinction between knowledge and belief is relative to the practices of a community. Researchers as well as mathematics students are truth makers.

SECOND-GRADE PROJECT

It should be clear from what has been said above that we consider models of children's construction of domain-specific mathematical knowledge to be essential but not sufficient for curriculum development and teacher education. In the remainder of the paper, we will focus on our attempts to develop cognitively based instructional activities and to facilitate teachers' development of their classroom practices.

Overview

Clinical interviews that concentrated on children's arithmetical knowledge and on their spatial memory and visualization abilities were conducted with beginning second graders during the first of the three years of the project. The findings of these interviews (Cobb & Wheatley, 1988) together with models of children's construction of arithmetical knowledge (Steffe et al., 1983; Steffe, Cobb, & von Glasersfeld, 1988) were used to guide the development of sample instructional activities.

During the second year, a teaching experiment was conducted in one second-grade public school classroom for the entire school year. The experiment had a strong pragmatic emphasis in that we were responsible for twenty children's mathematics instruction. Thus, we had to accommodate a variety of institutional constraints that reflect behaviorist assumptions while developing a form of practice compatible with constructivism. For example, we agreed to address all of the participating school corporation's objectives for second-grade mathematics. The primary rationale for these objectives was derived from current standardized testing practices. Naturally, we translated these objectives into our own terms. Thus, we attempted to achieve the objective that the children would be able to add and subtract two-digit numbers by encouraging them to construct their own efficient, conceptually based algorithms. We were also well aware that mean gains on standardized tests would weigh heavily in school corporation administrators' evaluations of the project. (But then they have obligations to their own constituencies.) It is for this reason that the paradox inherent in teaching is so real to us.

The test scores did rise satisfactorily and, as a consequence, twenty-four teachers are currently using the instructional activities in their classrooms during the third year of the project. Another constraint was introduced with the implementation of a state-mandated accountability program (the California Achievement Test). Under this program, a predetermined percentage of children who have the lowest scores (ranging from 8.8 percent to 15 percent depending on the source) will have to attend summer school for remediation and, if necessary, repeat second grade. Although the test scores have not been released at this time, reports from teachers and school principals are uniformly positive.

We mention these institutional constraints to emphasize that curriculum and teacher development lead to conflicts between value systems; what constitutes a sound mathematics education for children? The conflict is between the goals established for mathematics instruction and the desire to facilitate the individual children's construction of knowledge as they grow into wider cultural life. These situations do not have an established solution or right answer. Rather, they involve ethical and moral deliberation.

Relationship with Teachers

A classroom teacher who had taught second-grade mathematics "straight by the book" for fifteen years was a member of the project staff and taught all lessons in the course of the classroom teaching experiment. This practice of working closely with teachers is based on the view that educational innovations can be understood only by analyzing the instructional process as embodied in teachers' and students' interactions. We question the view that the relationship between teachers and researchers should be one in which researchers take teachers' problems, devise a solution, and then communicate the solution to teachers (Research Advisory Committee, National Council of Teachers of Mathematics, 1987). We consider that the constructivist theory of knowledge applies as much to ourselves and to teachers as to mathematics students. From this perspective, researchers and teachers have complimentary domains of expertise. Teachers, for example, have far richer experiences of interacting with children within the institutionalized constraints of the school. This wealth of experience is valuable, and we therefore attempt to construct a consensual domain with the project teachers. In the process of doing so, the teacher who participated in the teaching experiment had a profound influence on the course of the project.

The Classroom Teaching Experiment Methodology

The teaching experiment conducted in the classroom is a natural extension of the constructivist teaching experiment in which the researcher interacts with and attempts to guide the learning of a single child (Cobb & Steffe, 1983; Steffe, 1983). In our view, the two methodologies are appropriate for different phases of a research program (Cobb, 1986c). Both methodologies allow the researcher to focus on the critical moments when children make cognitive restructurings and develop increasingly powerful ways of knowing mathematics. In this regard, the methodologies do not suffer from the limitations of more routine methodologies in which "there exists strong evidence for a particular initial performance and a final one. However, there is usually no observation of the acquisition process itself" (Resnick, 1983, p. 28). In the case of the classroom teaching experiment, the restructurings occur as the children interact with the teacher and their peers rather than with the researcher. This allows the researcher to address a variety of related issues, the most important of which is to embed the children's construction of mathematical knowledge within the context of unfolding classroom life by coordinating psychological and anthropological perspectives.

The classroom teaching experiment also bears certain resemblances to a type of Soviet teaching experiment that Menchinskaya (1969) called a "macro scheme": "Changes are studied in a pupil's school activity and development as he [or she] makes the transition from one age level to another, from one level of instruction to another" (p. 5). However, there is a crucial difference between our approach and that of Soviet researchers. Typically, Soviet investigators construct curriculum materials before the experiment begins (for example, Davydov, 1975). We, in contrast, developed sample educational activities in the year preceding the experiment, but the specific activities used in the classroom were constructed, modified, and, when necessary, abandoned while the experiment was in progress. Consequently, formative evaluation, curriculum development, and the initial analyses of classroom life and individual children's mathematical activity were but different aspects of a single process. It is here that research and practice become so intertwined that it makes sense to separate them only for ease of explication.

Video recordings were made of every mathematics lesson during the school year using a single camera for whole class interactions and two cameras for small group interactions. During small group work, each camera focused on one of four selected pairs. It was therefore possible to record approximately half of each group's problem-solving activity throughout the year. Researchers, acting as participant observers, intervened only to ask clarifying questions that would aid the subsequent analysis. Additional data sources include videotaped clinical interviews conducted with all twenty children at the beginning, middle, and end of the school year, ethnographic field notes, copies of all the children's written work, the teacher's daily diary of her reflections, and audio recordings of open-ended interviews conducted with the teacher. A description of typical classroom life can be found in Cobb, Yackel, and Wood (1989) and Yackel, Cobb, and Wood (in press).

Development of Instructional Activities

Part of our rationale for both developing instructional activities and facilitating teachers' development stems from the belief that available instructional materials constrain possible forms of teaching practice. This view is compatible with Simon's (1988) recent evaluation of a constructivist mathematics teacher in-service program. He concluded that

> both elementary and secondary teachers, while being novices in constructivist teaching, are being put in a situation of having to create their own curricula. This is an overwhelming task ... Curriculum materials consistent with constructivist teaching must be developed. (p. 7)

We attempted to develop instructional activities that would facilitate forms of teaching compatible with constructivism and that would reflect our understanding of children's construction of arithmetical knowledge. From the psychological perspective, we view the process of learning mathematics as one in which students reorganize their activity in an attempt to resolve situations that they find problematic (where problematic is broadly defined to include experiences of interacting with others). We therefore used models of children's construction of arithmetical knowledge (Steffe et al., 1983; Steffe, Cobb, & von Glasersfeld, 1988) to both anticipate what might constitute problems for children at a variety of conceptual levels as they interpret possible instructional activities and how they might reorganize their activity to resolve their problems. The models can be used to generate anticipations of this sort, because they were originally developed to account for children's inferred mathematical experiences. In other words, the models do not account for children's mathematical behavior per se but rather for the inferred underlying experiences of children as they engage in mathematical activity. It is then children's inferred mathematical realities rather than classified solution strategies that constitute the 'data' to be explained. In our view, if we believe that students learn mathematics on the basis of their experiences, we need models that attempt to account for those experiences.

A basic assumption implicit in the models is that children come to experience apparently mind-independent mathematical objects by reflectively abstracting from and objectifying prior mathematical constructions. The root metaphor of these experiences is material physical reality (Bloor, 1976). To characterize the mathematical experiences of children before they have made these objectifications, one needs to talk about what it might be like before one can talk as a Platonist. This is the language of interpretivism. Here, the root metaphor is that of using a tool while interacting with physical reality (Polyani, 1962). We find value in the models developed by Steffe precisely because they attempt to capture the experiences of children before they have constructed number as an arithmetical object (that is, counters of perceptual, figural, motor, and verbal unit items) and ten as an objectified unit itself composed of ones (that is, ten as a numerical composite and as an abstract composite unit). Use of the interpretivist metaphor allowed us to consider what might be problematic in the experiences of children who are yet to objectify particular mathematical concepts.

A first characteristic of instructional activities, then, is that they make sense to, and can be solved by, children at qualitatively different conceptual levels. Some children might use the available manipulative materials, whereas others might produce relatively sophisticated, purely conceptual solutions. This approach gives children a large measure of control in individualizing their instruction and is compatible with intellectual autonomy as a goal of mathematics instruction (Kamii, 1985). In our view, problems cannot be given ready-made to children. Instead, problems arise for students as they attempt to achieve their goals in the classroom while interacting with others. Research evidence indicates that children are good judges of what they find problematic once classroom social norms have been renegotiated to encourage task-involvement rather than ego-involvement as the predominant form of motivation (Nicholls, 1983, 1989).

A second characteristic of the instructional activities concerns the relationship between conceptual and procedural knowledge. As Steiner (1987) noted, many of the short-lived reform movements and waves of fashion in mathematics education have ebbed and flowed between polarized emphases on conceptual understanding and procedural competency. Recent advances in cognitive science have brought the relationship between conceptual and procedural knowledge into sharper focus (Hiebert, 1986). It is generally agreed that young children enter school with a repertoire of self-generated algorithms and problem-solving strategies that express and are based on their conceptual understandings (Briars & Larkin, 1984; Carpenter, Hiebert, & Moser, 1983; Ginsburg, 1977; Riley, Greeno, & Heller, 1983; Steffe et al., 1983; Steffe, Cobb, & von Glasersfeld, 1988). Empirical findings indicate that as a consequence of school instruction in the early grades, the procedures that children construct become divorced from their conceptual knowledge (for example, Cobb, 1987; Hiebert & Lefevre, 1986; Silver, 1986). It is generally accepted that this is an outcome of traditional instructional practices in which students' informal ways of making meaning are given little attention. However, as Nesher (1986) observes, "no one has succeeded in demonstrating that understanding improves algorithmic performance" (p. 6). In other words, the shared belief among mathematics educators that one should first teach for understanding is without empirical support. Together with Nesher (1986) and Silver (1986), we suggest that the source of the difficulty might well be the way conceptual knowledge is opposed to procedural knowledge. Our fundamental contention is that even the process of constructing computational algorithms is a problem-solving activity. In particular, situations in which students' current algorithms lead to obstacles or contradictions are a crucial source of problems. The challenge of constructing a viable algorithm constitutes an opportunity to reorganize conceptual knowledge (Cobb, Wood, & Yackel, in press). In this view, conceptual and procedural developments should, ideally, go hand in hand. The relationship between the two is dialectical in that algorithms express conceptual knowledge and attempts to use current algorithms give rise to opportunities to construct new conceptual knowledge that informs more sophisticated algorithms.

The problem-center approach to materials development in which children are encouraged to construct their own increasingly efficient nonstandard computational algorithms represents our attempt to approach this ideal. The instructional activities we have developed cannot be partitioned into two sets, one designed to foster conceptual understanding and the other procedural competency. Our focus on what is problematic for children makes it possible to simultaneously consider potential conceptual and procedural advances.

A third characteristic of the instructional activities is that they address all traditional second-grade mathematics objectives in the sense of making it possible for children to achieve satisfactory test scores. The greatest challenge for us was to develop a sequence of activities that would make it possible for children to construct their own conceptually based computational algorithms and thus be able to produce correct answers to two-digit addition and substraction tasks. Our general strategy has been to first encourage children to build on their counting-based knowledge by developing thinking strategies (or derived-fact strategies) and elaborating their concepts of addition and subtraction. This is followed by activities designed to foster the construction of solution methods that involve multiple units (that is, units other than one). Finally, the children complete activities specifically designed to give them opportunities to construct increasingly sophisticated units of ten and computational algorithms. In sequencing activities in this way, we have attempted to view as aspects of a coherent developmental whole topics that are typically treated separately in textbook instruction (for example, basic facts, place value, money, elementary concepts of multiplication and division, and addition and subtraction algorithms).

A final characteristic of the instructional activities is that they make it possible for the whole class to sustain discussions about mathematics. In other words, the activities should be appropriate from the anthropological as well as the psychological perspective. Generally, interesting discussions occur when the children produce a variety of different solution methods that can be compared and contrasted or when they make what they call discoveries that they want to share with others. These features of the instructional activities are, of course, compatible with the requirements that they be conceptually appropriate and cater to individual differences. Further, from the anthropological perspective, mathematical truth emerges in the course of social interaction (that is, the anthropologist's concept of emergent meaning). We did not attempt to embed mathematical truths in the instructional activities by developing instructional representations. Given our epistemology, we are interested in emerging systems rather than delivery systems when it comes to matters of belief, knowledge, and truth.

Teacher Development

The approach we have adopted to teacher development is based on the premise that teachers, as much as mathematics students, construct their own ways of knowing. This, for us, implies that teachers should be encouraged to reorganize their pedagogical content knowledge and beliefs by resolving situations that they find problematic. We have already noted that knowledge constructed in this way need not take the form of a body of principles. Our goal is to help teachers develop ways of knowing that are appropriate for their purposes in the classroom. In other words, the contexts of pragmatic pedagogical reasoning and academic reasoning, within which formal models are constructed, might differ significantly. This speculation is compatible with the findings of investigations into pragmatic mathematical reasoning. For example, in an investigation of the mathematical practices of workers in a dairy, Scribner (1984) found that skilled practical thinking changed with the properties and conditions of a problem and, in this regard, is unlike the type of academic thinking that uses algorithms to solve all problems of a given type.

Our work with teachers involves an initial one week summer in-service institute followed by classroom visits and after-school working sessions. The basic goal of the summer institute is to help teachers consider whether aspects of their current practice might be problematic. Only then in our view will teachers have reason and motivation to attempt to reorganize their classroom practice during mathematics instruction (Wood, Cobb, & Yackel, 1990). To this end, we conducted several sessions with the goal of developing shared interpretations of video recordings of children's mathematical problem solving. The recordings were selected to provide teachers with an opportunity to question taken-for-granted assumptions about both the beliefs and mathematical knowledge that children construct in the course of typical textbook instruction. This approach is compatible with Peirce's (1958) contention that doubt is a prerequisite for the rejection of current belief.

As an example, we have become aware that the pedagogy of second-grade mathematics consists of a range of institutionalized practices whose implicit intent is to produce correct performance on a limited range of tasks. The instructional tasks used and the assessment questions posed are narrow in scope and use a variety of idiosyncratic conventions. In fact, the emphasis on iconic conventions is such that a mathematically competent adult not familiar with the text has difficulty in answering some of the tasks included in chapter tests because he or she simply does not know what the task is. Conversely, children can produce correct answers by learning a set of idiosyncratic conventions that have little, if anything, to do with mathematical understanding. The crucial point is that teachers almost uniformly take it for granted that children who give correct answers to these questions have constructed place value numeration in much the same way that they themselves have. In other words, this narrow range of stereotypical questions has been institutionalized as a true indicator of place value understanding. More generally, teachers take it as self-evident that children who complete a set of tasks correctly think in much the same way they themselves would when completing the same tasks. To challenge this belief, we present teachers with video recordings of children attempting textbook and nontextbook tasks. The nontextbook tasks are chosen to have face validity for the teacher. Teachers assume that children who can do the textbook tasks will also be able to complete the nontextbook tasks because they appear to involve the same concepts or skills that the children are assumed to have learned. In our experience teachers are shocked when they find that their taken-for-granted assumptions about children's learning are unwarranted. They begin to differentiate between correct performance and mathematical activity that expresses conceptual understanding. It is then that they question the adequacy of textbook instructional activities and are willing to experiment with activities designed to challenge students and give them opportunities to reorganize their current ways of thinking.

To complement activities designed to call into question some of their basic assumptions, the teachers participated in a simulation of the project classroom. We arranged to have eleven children from that classroom return for two hours each day during the institute. Institute participants observed instruction conducted by the project teacher and then worked one-on-one with a child to investigate his or her problem-solving methods. A discussion was then conducted during which teachers were encouraged to share their interpretations.

The remainder of the summer institute was devoted to developing a rationale for an alternative instructional approach, engaging in and reflecting on mathematical problem solving, discussing video recordings of both whole class discussions and small group work, and analyzing the instructional materials. At this point we gave straightforward answers to questions about the pragmatics of the instructional approach, focusing particularly on the process of initiating and guiding the renegotiation of classroom social norms for mathematics instruction. Our goal in being relatively prescriptive with regard to pragmatic issues involving classroom management and the negotiation of classroom norms was not to program teachers to do it in a specific way. Rather, it was to make it possible for teachers to concentrate on children's mathematical activity rather than on management issues when they began using the instructional activities in their classrooms. In effect, we were prescriptive so that the teachers' classrooms would be conducive learning environments for them as well as for their students during mathematics instruction. To clarify this aspect of our approach, we first discuss the crucial role of classroom social norms and then present several examples to illustrate the specific way in which pragmatic issues were dealt with.

By *classroom norms* we mean the taken-for-granted regularities or patterns implicit in classroom social interactions. The norms can be thought of as constituting the grammar of social interactions. They are generated by the unarticulated expectations that the teacher and students have for each other in particular situations and by the obligations they implicitly accept for their own activity. For example, the project teacher's expectations for the children during small group activities included that they work cooperatively to try to complete the activities, that they listen to and try to make sense of each other's problem-solving activity, and that they persist to figure out problems for themselves. The meaning of notions, such as working cooperatively, had to be negotiated by the teacher and children in concrete situations (Yackel, Cobb, & Wood, in press). In the process, the teacher modified her expectations and the children revised their obligations until at least temporary compatibility was achieved (Wood & Yackel, 1990). The process of mutually constructing social norms therefore involved the teacher and children establishing a fit between their respective obligations and expectations. It is this fit that, of course, makes possible the relatively smooth flow of classroom interactions.

The renegotiation of classroom social norms is crucial in that it is through this process that teachers influence children's beliefs during mathematics instruction (Cobb, Yackel, & Wood, 1989). Further, the mutual construction of appropriate classroom norms makes possible the development of intellectual autonomy and task-involvement as a form of motivation (Nicholls, 1989). This, in turn, means that teachers spend much less time monitoring general classroom activity and have more opportunities to observe and interact with children as they engage in informal, conceptually based mathematical activity. These observations constitute prime opportunities for teachers to learn from their students, in that much of what they see is problematic or surprising to them (Wood, Cobb, & Yackel, 1990). Thus, we contend that teachers as well as students learn in the course of instruction and consider that teachers' learning is an essential aspect of any model of teachers' cognitions. Failure to initiate and guide the mutual construction of appropriate classroom social norms greatly diminishes opportunities for teachers to learn from their students' mathematical activity.

One aspect of our relative directness with regard to the renegotiation of classroom norms was to show and then discuss video recordings of specific situations from the project classroom. For example, at one point during the school year the teacher initiated a class discussion about how one feels when struggling with a problem if someone says, "That's easy." She concluded the discussion by saying that "From now on those two words are not allowed in this classroom during math." In the course of discussions, the project teacher explained her rationale for this and other interventions and fielded questions about hypothetical cases generated by the teachers. In general, the recordings featured episodes in which the teacher capitalized on specific situations where children either met or failed to meet obligations. These instances constitute concrete cases in which the teacher initiated the renegotiation of classroom norms. A second example illustrates the level of specificity with which we dealt with classroom management issues during the institute. During some of the problem-solving activities, the children used cards with one problem statement per card. When a group completed a problem they traded their card for another. The trading process was greatly facilitated if one location in the classroom was designated as the trading center. There children returned the problem card they had completed and picked up another card. We specifically suggested to teachers that they use a trading center and that they permit only one child from each group to go to the center to return and pick up cards. By doing so we alleviated the need for teachers to figure out such managerial strategies for themselves. Likewise, many of the instructional activities involved the use of an overhead projector. The project teacher worked out a number of techniques to increase the efficiency of projector use. These were discussed directly with the workshop participants as techniques they might wish to follow.

In relating our approach to the literature on teachers' cognitions, we note that the findings of several studies indicate that teachers' beliefs (Brown & Cooney, in press; Cooney, 1985; Thompson, 1985) and pedagogical content knowledge (Peterson et al., 1987) influence their classroom practice. We suggest that the relationship also holds in the reverse direction: Experiences of interacting with students in the classroom profoundly influence teachers' pedagogical content knowledge and beliefs. In other words, like the relationship between conceptual and procedural knowledge, the relationship between teachers' knowledge and beliefs and their practice is dialectical. We question the assumption that interventions designed to modify teachers' beliefs and knowledge outside the context of classroom practice is the most effective way to influence that practice (cf. Bush, 1986; Cooney, 1985). For this reason, we did not discuss models of early number learning with the teachers before they began to use the instructional activities. Our teacher colleague convinced us on the basis of her own experiences that her fellow teachers would not appreciate the relevance of the models to their classroom practice at that point. It was when the teachers began to use the problem-centered activities that they encountered problematic situations. They came to realize that they had an inadequate knowledge of children's mathematics activity and actively wanted to learn about it. We therefore conducted a series of working sessions that focused on various methods children use as they attempt to solve arithmetical activities. By observing and discussing videotapes, the teachers developed mutually acceptable interpretations of children's mathematical activity. The solution methods discussed were dovetailed with the instructional activities that the teachers were using. Initial sessions dealt with counting by ones and thinking strategies, whereas the concern in later sessions was with units of ten, computational algorithms, and multiplicative and divisional concepts.

We have repeatedly stressed parallels between teachers' and students' learning. To continue this theme, the teachers as well as the students were organized into small groups of three or four that meet weekly to discuss their problems, concerns, and insights. In addition, approximately once every two weeks, a member of the project staff visits the classroom of each of the twenty-four teachers who are currently using the instructional activities. The primary purposes are to address teachers' pragmatic concerns (for example, how to involve all children in discussions) and to help them make aspects of their routinized, taken-for-granted practice problematic (for example, responding to children's solutions in a subtle but nonetheless evaluative manner). In attempting to raise problems rather than tell teachers what to do, we have intellectual autonomy as a goal for teachers as well as students. In this regard, we are gratified to find that the teachers are increasingly relying on their own judgments when both selecting from the available materials and deciding which activities to discuss as a class on the basis of their observations. It would seem that they are becoming curriculum constructors who select from the overabundance of available instructional activities to meet their students' needs. We suggest that teachers' increasing commitment to the problem-centered instructional approach is attributable in part to the control they have over their own learning and practice.

CONCLUDING REMARKS

Finally, we return to the paradox of teaching. The teachers' growing sense of autonomy is related to our attempts to cope with the tension between the needs of individual children and the institutional constraints as best we could when developing the instructional activities. It was the project staff rather than the teachers who were accountable. From the teachers' perspective, they could concentrate on children's learning and, to the extent that they trusted us, assume that test scores would take care of themselves. In a sense, the teachers did not cover content as in textbook instruction. Instead, they attempted to engage children in meaningful mathematical activity. Further, they were not under the obligation of ensuring that all children made certain predetermined mathematical constructions when they used particular instructional activities. This reduced the possibility that they would develop the types of routines documented by Voigt (1985). What is traditionally called content — mathematics as cultural knowledge — was negotiated and institutionalized by classroom intellecutal communities as teachers and children interacted about mathematics. In the very process of constituting and regenerating these communities, the teachers and children as cognitive individuals learned from each other. It is in this sense that the psychological and anthropological perspectives are distinct yet interdependent.

REFERENCES

Addison-Wesley Mathematics Teacher's Resource Book, Book 2 (1987). Menlo Park, CA: Addison-Wesley.

Balacheff, N. (1986). Cognitive versus situational analysis of problem-solving behavior. *For the Learning of Mathematics, 6*(3), 10–12.

Barnes, D., & Todd, F. (1977). *Communicating and learning in small groups.* London: Routledge & Kegan Paul.

Bauersfeld, H. (1980). Hidden dimensions in the so-called reality of a mathematics classroom. *Educational Studies in Mathematics, 11,* 23–41.

————. (1988). Interaction, construction, and knowledge: Alternative perspectives for mathematics education. In T. Cooney & D. Grouws (Eds.), *Research agenda for mathematics education: Effective mathematics teaching.* Reston, VA: National Council of Teachers of Mathematics.

Bernstein, R. J. (1983). *Beyond objectivism and relativism: Science, hermeneutics, and praxis.* Philadelphia: University of Pennsylvania Press.

Bishop, A. (1985). The social construction of meaning — a significant development for mathematics education? *For the Learning of Mathematics, 5*(1), 24–28.

Bloor, D. (1976). *Knowledge and social imagery.* London: Routledge & Kegan Paul.

————. (1983). *Wittgenstein: A social theory of knowledge.* New York: Columbia University Press.

Brannigan, A. (1981). *The social basis of scientific discovery.* Cambridge: Cambridge University Press.

Briars, D. J., & Larkin, J. H. (1984). An integrated model of skill in solving elementary word problems. *Cognition and Instruction, 1,* 245–296.

Brown, S., & Cooney, T. (in press). The relevance of beliefs for mathematics teacher education. In W. R. Houston (Ed.), *Handbook of research on teacher education*. New York: Macmillan.

Bruner, J. (1986). *Actual minds, possible worlds*. Cambridge: Harvard University Press.

Bush, W. S. (1986). Preservice teachers' sources of decisions in teaching secondary mathematics. *Journal for Research in Mathematics Education, 17,* 21–30.

Carpenter, T. P., & Fennema, E. (1988). *Research and cognitively guided instruction*. Madison, WI: National Center for Research in Mathematical Sciences Education.

Carpenter, T. P., Hiebert, J., & Moser, J. M. (1983). The effect of instruction on children's solutions of addition and subtraction word problems. *Educational Studies in Mathematics, 14,* 55–72.

Carraher, T. N., & Carraher, D. W. (1987). *Mathematics as personal and social activity*. Paper presented at the International Conference on Success or Failure? The Child's Development at School, Poitiers, France.

Clark, C. M. (1988). Asking the right question about teacher preparation: Contributions of research on teacher thinking. *Educational Researcher, 17*(2), 5–12.

Clark, C. M., & Lampert, M. (1986). The study of teacher thinking: Implications for teachers education. *Journal of Teacher Education, 37*(5), 27–31.

Clark, C. M., & Peterson, P. L. (1986). Teachers' thought processes. In M. C. Wittrock (Ed.), *Handbook of research on teaching* (3rd ed., pp. 255–296). New York: Macmillan.

Cobb, P. (1985). Two children's anticipations, beliefs, and motivations. *Educational Studies in Mathematics, 16,* 111–126.

Cobb, P. (1986a). Concrete can be abstract: A case study. *Educational Studies in Mathematics, 17,* 37–48.

Cobb, P. (1986b). Contexts, goals, beliefs, and learning mathematics. *For the Learning of Mathematics, 6*(2), 2–9.

Cobb, P. (1986c). Clinical interviewing in the context of research programs. In G. Lappan & R. Even (Eds.), *Proceedings of the eighth annual meeting of PME-NA: Plenary speeches and symposium*. East Lansing, MI: Michigan State University.

Cobb, P. (1987). An investigation of young children's academic arithmetic contexts. *Educational Studies in Mathematics, 18,* 109–124.

Cobb, P. (1989). Experiential, cognitive, and anthropological perspectives in mathematics education. *For the Learning of Mathemaics, 9*(2), 32–42.

Cobb, P., & Steffe, L. P. (1983). The constructivist researcher as teacher and model builder. *Journal for Research in Mathematics Education, 14,* 83–94.

Cobb, P., & Wheatley, G. H. (1988). Children's initial understandings of ten. *Focus on Learning Problems in Mathematics, 10*(3), 1–28.

Cobb, P., Wood, T., & Yackel, E. (in press). Learning through problem solving: A constructivist approach to second grade mathematics. In E. von Glasersfeld (Ed.), *Constructivism in mathematics education.* Dordrecht, Holland: Reidel.

Cobb, P., Yackel, E., & Wood, T. (1989). Young children's emotional acts while engaging in mathematical problem solving. In D. B. McLeod & V. M. Adams (Eds.), *Affect and mathematical problem solving: A new perspective* (pp. 117–148). New York: Springer-Verlag.

Confrey, J. (1984, April). *An examination of the conceptions of mathematics of young women in high school.* Paper presented at the annual meeting of the American Educational Research Association, New Orleans.

Confrey, J. (1987, July). *The current state of constructivist thought in mathematics education.* Paper presented at the annual meeting of the International Group for the Psychology of Mathematics Education, Montreal.

Cooney, T. J. (1985). A beginning teacher's view of problem solving. *Journal for Research in Mathematics Education, 16,* 324–336.

D'Ambrosio, U. (1985). Ethnomathematics and its place in the history and pedagogy of mathematics. *For the Learning of Mathematics, 5*(1), 44–48.

Davis, P. J., & Hersh, R. (1981). *The mathematical experience.* Boston: Houghton Mifflin.

Davydov, V. V. (1975). The psychological characteristics of the "prenumerical" period of mathematics instruction. In L. P. Steffe (Ed.), *Soviet studies in the psychology of learning and teaching mathematics* (Vol. 7, pp. 190–205). Stanford, CA: School Mathematics Study Group.

Doyle, W. (1983). Academic work. *Review of Educational Research, 53,* 159–199.

Eisenhart, M. A. (1988). The ethnographic research tradition and mathematics education research. *Journal for Research in Mathematics Education, 19,* 99–114.

Gadamer, H. G. (1986). *Truth and method.* New York: Crossroad.

Ginsburg, H. (1977). *Children's arithmetic: The learning process.* New York: Van Nostrand.

Hiebert, J. I., (Ed.). (1986). *Conceptual knowledge and procedural knowledge: The case of mathematics.* Hillsdale, NJ: Lawrence Erlbaum Associates.

Hiebert, J., & Lefevre, P. (1986). Conceptual and procedural knowledge in mathematics: An introductory analysis. In J. I. Hiebert (Ed.), *Conceptual and procedural knowledge: The case of mathematics* (pp. 1–27). Hillsdale, NJ: Lawrence Erlbaum Associates.

Hundeide, K. (1985). The tacit background of children's judgments. In J. V. Wertsch (Ed.), *Culture, communication, and cognition* (pp. 306–322). Cambridge: Cambridge University Press.

Kamii, C. (1985). *Young children reinvent arithmetic: Implications of Piaget's theory.* New York: Teachers College Press.

Labinowicz, E. (1985). *Learning from children.* Menlo Park, CA: Addison-Wesley.

Lakatos, I. (1976). *Proofs and refutations.* Cambridge: Cambridge University Press.

Lampert, M. L. (1985). How teachers teach. *Harvard Educational Review, 55,* 229–246.

Lave, J. (1984, April). *Paper and pencil skills in the real world.* Paper presented at the annual meeting of the American Educational Research Association, New Orleans.

Levina, R. E. (1981). L. S. Vygotsky's ideas about the planning function of speech in children. In J. V. Wertsch (Ed.), *The concept of activity in Soviet psychology* (pp. 279–299). Armonk, NY: Sharpe.

Maturana, H. R. (1978). Biology of language: The epistemology of reality. In G. A. Miller & E. Lennenberg (Eds.), *Psychology and biology of language and thought: Essays in honor in Eric Lennenberg* (pp. 27–63). New York: Academic Press.

Menchinskaya, N. A. (1969). Fifty years of soviet instructional psychology. In J. Kilpatrick & I. Wirszup (Eds.), *Soviet studies in the psychology of learning and teaching mathematics* (Vol. 1, pp. 5–27). Stanford, CA: School Mathematics Study Group.

Nesher, P. (1986). Are mathematical understanding and algorithmic performances related? *For the Learning of Mathematics, 6*(3), 2–9.

Nicholls, J. G. (1983). Conceptions of ability and achievement motivation: A theory and its implications for education. In S. G. Paris, G. M. Olson, & W. H. Stevenson (Eds.), *Learning and motivation in the classroom* (pp. 211–237). Hillsdale, NJ: Lawrence Erlbaum Associates.

―――. (1989). *The competitive ethos and democratic education.* Cambridge: Harvard University Press.

Pask, G. (1985). Problematic situations. *Cybernetic, 1,* 79–87.

Peirce, C. S. (1935). *Collected papers of Charles Sanders Peirce* (Vol. 5, C. Hartshorne & P. Weiss, Eds.). Cambridge: Harvard University Press.

Peirce, C. S. (1958). The fixation belief. In P. P. Weiner (Ed.), *Values in a universe of chance: Selected writings of Charles S. Peirce* (pp. 92–113). Stanford: Stanford University Press.

Perret-Clermont, A. N. (1980). *Social interaction and cognitive development in children.* New York: Academic Press.

Peterson, P. L., Fennema, E., Carpenter, T. P., & Loef, M. (1987). *Teachers' pedagogical content beliefs in mathematics.* Paper presented at the meeting of the American Educational Research Association, Washington, DC.

Polyani, M. (1962). *Personal knowledge.* Chicago: University of Chicago Press.

Research Advisory Committee, National Council of Teachers of Mathematics (1987, April). *Highlights in research activities in mathematics education 1986.* Paper presented at the annual meeting of the National Council of Teachers of Mathematics, Anaheim, CA.

Resnick, L. B. (1983). Towards a cognitive theory of instruction. In S. G. Paris, G. M. Olson, & W. H. Stevenson (Eds.), *Learning and motivation in the classroom* (pp. 5–38). Hillsdale, NJ: Lawrence Erlbaum Associates.

Resnick, L. B. (1987). Learning in and out of school. *Educational Researcher, 16*(9), 13–20.

Riley, M. S., Greeno, J. G., & Heller, J. I. (1983). Development of children's problem-solving ability in mathematics. In H. P. Ginsburg (Ed.), *The development of mathematical thinking* (pp. 153–196). New York: Academic Press.

Romberg, T. A., & Carpenter, T. P. (1986). Research on teaching and learning mathematics: Two disciplines of scientific enquiry. In M. C. Wittrock (Ed.), *Handbook of research on teaching* (3rd ed., pp. 850–873). New York: Macmillan.

Saxe, G. B. (1988, January). *The interplay between children's learning in formal and informal social contexts.* Paper presented at the conference on the Scientific Practice of Science Education, Berkeley, California.

Schoenfeld, A. H. (1985). *Mathematical problem solving.* Orlando, FL: Academic Press.

Schon, D. A. (1983). *The reflective practitioner.* New York: Basic Books.

Scribner, S. (1984). Studying working intelligence. In B. Rogoff & J. Lave (Eds.), *Everyday cognition: Its development in social context* (pp. 9–40). Cambridge: Harvard University Press.

Sigel, I. E. (1981). Social Experience in the development of representational thought: Distancing theory. In I. E. Sigel, D. M. Brodzinsky, & R. M. Golinkoff (Eds.), *New directions in Piagetian theory and practice* (pp. 203–217). Hillsdale, NJ: Lawrence Erlbaum Associates.

Silver, E. A. (1986). Using conceptual and procedural knowledge: A focus on relationships. In J. Hiebert (Ed.), *Conceptual and procedural knowledge: The case of mathematics* (pp. 181–198). Hillsdale, NJ: Lawrence Erlbaum Associates.

Simon, H. A. (1976). *Administrative behavior* (3rd ed.). New York: The Free Press.

Simon, M. A. (1988, July). *Formative evaluation of a constructivist mathematics teacher inservice program.* Paper presented at the meeting of the International Group for the Psychology of Mathematics Education, Veszprem, Hungary.

Smedslund, J. (1977). Piaget's psychology in practice. *British Journal of Educational Psychology, 47,* 1–6.

Steffe, L. P. (1983). The teaching experiment methodology in a constructivist research program. In M. Zweng, T. Green, J. Kilpatrick, H. Pollak, & M. Suydam (Eds.), *Proceedings of the Fourth International Congress on Mathematical Education.* Boston: Birkhauser.

Steffe, L. P. (1987, April). *Principles of mathematical curriculum design in early childhood teacher education.* Paper presented at the annual meeting of the American Educational Research Association, Washington, DC.

Steffe, L. P., Cobb, P., & von Glasersfeld, E. (1988). *Construction of arithmetical meanings and strategies.* New York: Springer-Verlag.

Steffe, L. P., von Glasersfeld, E., Richards, J., & Cobb, P. (1983). *Children's counting types: Philosophy, theory, and application*. New York: Praeger Scientific.

Steiner, H. G. (1987). A systems approach to mathematics education. *Journal for Research in Mathematics Education, 18,* 46–52.

Thompson, P. (1985). Experience, problem solving, and learning mathematics: Considerations in developing mathematics curricula. In E. A. Silver (Ed.), *Teaching and learning mathematical problem solving: Multiple research perspectives* (pp. 198–236). Hillsdale, NJ: Lawrence Erlbaum Associates.

Toulmin, S. (1983). The construal of reality: Criticism in modern and post modern science. In W. J. T. Mitchell (Ed.), *The politics of interpretation* (pp. 99–117). Chicago: University of Chicago Press.

Voigt, J. (1985). Patterns and routines in classroom interaction. *Recherches en Didactique des Mathématiques, 6,* 69–118.

von Glasersfeld, E. (1983). Learning as a constructive activity. In N. Herscovics & J. C. Bergeron (Eds.), *Proceedings of the Fifth Annual Meeting of the North American Chapter of the International Group for the Psychology of Mathematics Education* (Vol. 1, pp. 41–69). Montréal: Université de Montreal, Faculté de Science de l'Éducation.

Wood, T., Cobb, P., & Yackel, E. (1990). The contextual nature of teaching: Mathematics and reading instruction in one second-grade classroom. *Elementary School Journal, 90*(5), 497–513.

Yackel, E., Cobb, P., & Wood, T. (in press). Small group interactions as a source of learning opportunities in second grade mathematics. *Journal for Research in Mathematics Education Monograph*.

Wood, T., & Yackel, E. (1990). The development of collaborative dialogue within small group interactions. In L. P. Steffe & T. Wood (Eds.), *Transforming children's mathematics education: Internation perspectives* (pp. 244–252). Hillsdale, NJ: Lawrence Erlbaum Associates.

5

Connecting Mathematical Teaching and Learning*

Magdalene Lampert

What sort of work is entailed in teaching mathematics for understanding in a school classroom? What does students' understanding look like in the social context of the public school? These questions about mathematics teaching and learning have guided the research and development project I have been conducting over the last four years. They are intended to connect research on learning with research on teaching by examining teaching and learning as two activities that occur together in the context of a classroom, and by analyzing how they might work together to produce students' understanding of mathematics.

The method I have chosen for this inquiry is unusual, and one of my research interests has been to learn about the method itself. I have been experimenting with a new role — that of teacher-scholar — to find out about new ways of constructing the relationship between scholarship and practice in education (Carnegie Forum on Education and the Economy, 1986; Holmes Group, 1986; Lortie, 1975). This role has been imagined as a novel way to conduct research which might be more accessible to practitioners, but it also has a more direct teacher education function, in

---

*This work was supported by the Spencer Foundation through the National Academy of Education and by Michigan State University through the Institute for Research on Teaching.

that the teaching is observed by preservice and practicing teachers who are concerned with teaching mathematics for understanding. This is a messier approach to scholarship and its dissemination than conducting studies in more controlled circumstances and then applying the findings, but it seems to have some potential to add to our knowledge about how expertise is acquired, both in mathematics and in teaching (Ball, in press; Florio & Clark, 1984; Gelman, 1986; Ginsburg & Yamamoto, 1986; Greeno, 1986; Shulman, 1988).

I have taught fourth- and fifth-grade mathematics during the past six years, collecting data on both teaching and learning during three of those years. These data include audiotapes of lessons for six months, videotapes of two curriculum units, an observer's records of speech and visual communication during lessons (kept at least three times a week over three years), notebooks in which students do their daily work (including writing and drawing they do to represent their thinking), and students' homework papers. Lessons are described in detailed field notes, including descriptions of how lessons and units were planned and implemented as well as initial analyses of the planning process itself, the lessons as they were taught, and students' work. These data are further analyzed using triangulation among different data sources and constant comparison within and between lessons. Collaborative analyses of lessons are carried out with educational psychologists, sociolinguists, and mathematicians; the lessons are observed in the classroom setting and recorded and analyzed by each observer using methodological tools and theories about knowledge drawn from his or her own discipline. Post hoc descriptions of several elements of the process of teaching mathematics for understanding have been produced based on these analyses, using theoretical frameworks drawn from philosophies of pedagogy, the psychology of cognition, and the mathematical structure of lesson content and student ideas.

In this process, the corpus of data is treated as a text to be analyzed, and the analysis is interactive with the process of developing new instructional methods and curriculum materials. Analyzing these data represents an attempt to unlock the tangled web of human activity in the classroom, where activity is carried on for multiple purposes other than doing research (Geertz, 1973). This method of analysis is what is sometimes referred to as "textual exegesis." The use of this method assumes that there are multiple ways to interpret any action, and that levels of meaning are confounded and sometimes in conflict (Hammersly, 1979; Taylor, 1979). This approach fits with the observation that teaching is a task that involves managing multiple and often contradictory goals (Berlak & Berlak, 1981; Jackson, 1968; Lampert, 1985a; Lortie, 1975). The purpose of such interpretive research is not to determine whether general propositions about learning or teaching are true or false, but to further our understanding of the character of these particular kinds of human activity. It is a narrative rather than a logico-scientific tradition of scholarship (Bruner, 1986).

SOME TASKS OF TEACHING FOR UNDERSTANDING

In this paper, two areas of this research program are examined to explore the question of what is entailed in teaching mathematics for understanding, and understanding mathematics in school: *choosing and posing problems*, and *developing tools for communication* between teacher and learners.[1] The analysis of the character of the teaching that is involved in these tasks is both rhetorical and empirical, including theoretical arguments for a particular kind of practice as well as reports on what happened when a particular practice was implemented in my classroom. The purpose of this analysis is (1) to conceptualize what teachers need to do to teach for understanding; that is, to define and analyze tasks that would not be a part of the teacher's job if he or she were concerned only about having students learn rules for doing computation or the definitions of mathematical terms and (2) to examine the appropriateness of this kind of teaching in the context of everyday public school practice. The conceptualization, in this case, is created in a zigzag fashion between scholarship and practice.

What is mathematical knowledge, and what does it imply for pedagogy?

Commonly, mathematics is associated with certainty, with knowing, with being able to get the right answer quickly (Ball, 1988; Schoenfeld, 1985; Stodolsky, 1988). These cultural assumptions are shaped by school experience, in which doing mathematics means remembering and applying the correct rule when the teacher asks a question, and mathematical truth is determined when the answer is ratified by the teacher. These beliefs about how to do mathematics and what it means to know it in school are acquired through years of watching, listening, and practicing. The conjecture with which I enter the classroom as a teacher is that teaching and learning for understanding involve a different sort of communication between teachers and students about mathematics than that which is found in traditional classrooms; it requires that both teacher and students redefine what counts as mathematical knowledge (Cazden, 1988; Hawkins, 1974). In mathematics, authority comes from agreeing on shared assumptions and reasoning about their consequences (Kramer, 1970). If teaching and learning are going to proceed with this view of knowledge rather than the one more commonly held, then, in order to teach mathematics, teachers need to make reasoned connections between what students assume about the structure of some mathematical domain and what they want them to learn. If they are successful, students will make reasoned connections between what they already know and the new material in order to learn mathematics.

My argument about how teachers and students need to communicate to define the meaning of mathematical knowing is primarily based on epistemological analyses of how new knowledge is established in the discipline, and theories of knowledge that locate meaning in the shared assumptions of the community of discourse (Berger & Luckmann, 1987). In mathematics, new knowledge is produced by testing assertions in a reasoned argument; in a community of discourse, people agree upon a set of assumptions, make generalizations about a given domain, and then explore the boundaries of the domain to which the generalizations apply (Davis & Hersch, 1987; Lakatos, 1976; Polya, 1954). Mathematics is about representing one structure in terms of another and figuring out what relationships obtain among elements of structures (Kaput, 1987). The program of research being considered here is designed to examine whether this way of thinking about disciplinary knowledge can describe the classroom interaction between teacher and students in school mathematics lessons.

If the process of coming to know mathematics in the classroom is going to have some relationship to the process of coming to know mathematics in the discipline, then teaching will involve getting students to reveal and examine the assumptions they are making about mathematical structures, and it will involve presenting new material in a way that enables them to consider the reasonability of their own and teacher's assertions. Lessons will be in the form of a mathematical argument, which students accept or reject on the basis of their own reasoning. One way to conduct such lessons is to choose and pose problems that create a context within which students will be inclined to reveal the assumptions they have about how a piece of mathematics can be structured. If these problems and their solutions are to be the setting for students and teachers to engage in mathematical argument, both teachers and students need to be able to use language and symbols to communicate their assumptions and prove or refute their own and others' assertions. Choosing and using "good problems" and instituting appropriate means of classroom communication can be thought of as two of the tasks that teachers need to do to teach mathematics.

I explore these tasks below, connecting inquiry about teaching with inquiry about the nature of mathematical understanding. My analysis provides some useful comparisons with the Cognitively Guided Instruction (CGI) project on which the Wisconsin model is based (Carpenter, et al., 1988; Carpenter & Fennema, 1988). The CGI project pedagogy is based on cognitive research, whereas mine is derived from an analysis of mathematical knowledge and discourse. They have many points in common. Each has important strengths, and each has weaknesses that correspond to its strengths.

Choosing and Using "Good Problems" to Create a Safe and Productive Learning Environment

"Using only two kinds of coins, make $1.00 with nineteen coins." This problem is typical of the sorts of problems I have used to engage students at the fourth- and fifth-grade levels in mathematical discourse. Such problems provoke teacher-student discussion and reveal how the student is thinking about the principles underlying some procedure that the teacher wants the student to learn. Constructing lessons around such problems is one way to structure teacher-student interaction that communicates to students what is important in doing mathematics: developing and defending strategies, making hypotheses, or what Lakatos (1976) calls "conscious guessing," and rising to the challenge of articulating and defending the knowledge of mathematical principles that lead up to one's guess.

What are the attributes that make this a good problem for teaching mathematics in a way that supports students' coming to understand mathematics? First, it has the potential to create a learning environment in which students are inclined to express their thinking about the mathematical structures underlying computational procedures. Coins are a safe domain in which to elicit students' participation in problem solving because working with coins involves a familiar set of relationships. But from the perspective of a teacher with an instructional agenda, such problems have a second important characteristic. They are productive in the sense that they have the potential to lead students into unfamiliar and important mathematical territory and, in particular, to lead them into territory that relates to the curricular agenda in the fourth grade.

In the familiar domain of coins, students have some experience with taking numbers apart and putting them back together again in different ways, and so their knowledge is secure. They know, and they can prove, that two quarters equal five dimes, six nickels equal three dimes, and so on, and these are the kinds of mathematical relationships one needs to know about in order to solve this kind of problem. These equalities can be shown to be true by the concrete act of trading: in the first case, both collections of coins can be shown to equal fifty pennies, and in the second case, thirty. Students can securely make conjectures about these relationships because they have a ready means to prove that their conjectures are true (Balachef, 1987). Working on the coin problem, students articulate what they know to be true, and make it possible for that knowledge to be abstracted and connected with other sorts of problem solving involving the same mathematical principles (Greeno, Riley, & Gelman, 1984). The conventional procedure, and any other efficient procedure for multiplying large numbers, involves using the distributive law, just as solving coin problems does, and it is here that the teacher can connect, in her teaching, what students bring to the learning of mathematics with the school's instructional agenda.

Beginning with a problem in a familiar domain, with the intention of extending the principles that apply there into other domains that are similar but more abstract, is a way in which teacher and students can communicate in what Vygotsky (1978) calls the students' "zone of proximal development." Good problems will elicit students' assumptions about how some piece of mathematics works, and in the public discourse of the classroom, these assumptions can be tested in new, less familiar domains introduced by the teacher. Good problems thus open up the possibility of moving into new territory while at the same time containing the tools with which students can check the legitimacy of their assertions themselves. As students talk about the reasoning they use to solve the more familiar problems, the teacher finds language that can later be used to introduce parallel structures in the less familiar domain. Constructing this interaction in such a way as to enable students to learn to understand mathematics involves attending to students' acquisition of two kinds of knowledge: knowledge of mathematical principles and the structures they support, or what might be called "content"; and knowing the form of discourse by which those principles can be shown to be true, which Schoenfeld (1985) calls the students' "mathematical epistemology." Students need to work in a domain where they can prove to themselves, to their peers, and to their teacher that what they are doing is reasonable so that they can learn about what kind of knowledge mathematics is. If students are to learn that mathematical principles are true, not by virtue of the teachers' authority, but by virtue of reasoned argument in a community of discourse, then they need experience with mathematical forms of legitimation (Green, 1971; Scheffler, 1965). Posing problems in a domain whose constraints are familiar (like coins) provides an environment in which students can find out for themselves whether their answers are correct.

In a classroom exploration of problems like: "Make $1.00 out of nineteen coins of only two types,"[2] fourth-grade students were able to reason with the principles of additive composition, commutativity, associativity, place value, and distributivity (Lampert, 1986a, 1986b). In later lessons with these students, analogies were made between coin problems and strategies for multidigit multiplication. In the case of coins, the legitimacy of mathematical principles was established concretely by talking about trading. When students were trying to make $1.00 using only nickels and dimes, they experimented with different ways of adjusting the possible combinations to get multiple solutions, thus asserting and practicing rules and relationships about the operations of addition and multiplication, and how they could be combined in the distributive law. Their arguments about legitimate ways of taking numbers apart and putting them back together were based on checking with a known set of relationships among imagined or real familiar objects. Knowledge about relationships among numbers in the domain of coins helped children argue among themselves and with their teacher about why the strategies they were using were appropriate. In the course of doing this kind of arguing, the students revealed to themselves and to their teacher a way of thinking about the big mathematical ideas that underlie their activity. In mathematical terms, these students were making hypotheses about relationships among quantities that they thought should be true, and then refuting them or proving that they were true using the materials. From the teacher's perspective, they were revealing an appropriate starting point for future lessons.

Problems like these are what Kilpatrick, following Frederikson (1984), called "structured problems requiring productive thinking" (Kilpatrick, 1987, p. 134). They imply criteria for testing the correctness of the solution, but they are not solved by the simple application of a known algorithm. This allows for multiple routes to a solution, and puts the solver in the position of devising all or part of the solution procedure. The student is responsible for figuring out how to solve the problem as well as finding the solution. It is the strategies, rather than the answers, that are the site of the mathematical thinking, and it is these strategies that reveal the assumptions a student is making about how mathematics works. When students do coin problems, they exhibit a variety of ways to take numbers apart, operate on them, and put them back together again, but their knowledge (like the knowledge of Scribner's milkmen) is limited to a domain whose constraints are more particular than the constraints that obtain in the domain of natural numbers (Scribner, 1984). Making such problems part of the classroom conversation means that the teacher can refer back to this domain-related knowledge to raise questions about how it might be extended into other domains, using language about numerical relationships that is familiar to students.

Another example of this sort of problem with which I have experimented in fifth-grade lessons is the "betweenness game" played with decimal numbers (Lampert, 1990). In this game, the teacher writes a number on the blackboard, and the class is challenged to come up with a smaller number.[3] These first two numbers establish the initial boundaries, and for the rest of the game, students assert their ideas about what number will be between numbers defining smaller and smaller intervals. For example, if the teacher initially writes ".5" on the board, and the first student to speak asserts that ".3" is smaller, the problem for the class now becomes finding a number between .5 and .3. The in-between number—say .35—becomes a new boundary, and the teacher erases one of the earlier numbers, so the problem then becomes finding a number between .3 and .35. If a student volunteers ".34," the teacher might erase .3, and then the problem is to find a number between .34 and .35. In the assertions they made about betweenness as they played this game in my class, students expressed their hypotheses about how decimal numbers work and how they can be ordered. As they argued about the legitimacy of their assertions with their peers, they called upon the principles that underlie the structure of decimal numbers, and they got practice in applying these principles in a problem-solving setting. They touched on big mathematical ideas as they recognized, in the competition to produce "between" numbers, that there are infinitely many numbers between two decimal numbers, and that they can be produced by using more and more decimal places. Again, they made their understanding public in an area where the teacher had an instructional agenda, while doing a problem whose structure had the capacity to elicit their understanding.

A third example of the sort of problem with which I have experimented to elicit students' understanding in a familiar realm so that I could take them into mathematical territory, was in the area of rates and ratios (Lampert, 1985b). Watching a video about a sailing ship risking disaster because of an electrical failure, students saw the captain throw a piece of bread over the side of the boat, and then use a stopwatch to determine how many seconds it took for the boat to pass the bread. Having completed this procedure, the captain announced how fast the boat was traveling in knots, enabling him to estimate the boat's position in relation to a nearby reef. The first problem for the class to solve was figuring out how he did that; then they were asked to speculate on what he would have said about the speed if the boat had gone by the bread more quickly or more slowly, or if the boat had been larger or smaller than the one in the film. Students drew pictures and acted out various time, speed, and distance scenarios as they argued with one another about whether a change in conditions would have the effect of increasing or decreasing the calculated speed. By manipulating familiar variables in a familiar context — boats and bread — they made conjectures about the more abstract structure of relationships in direct and inverse proportions within the time, speed, and distance formula. Getting students to reveal their knowledge about rates and ratios within public discourse enabled me, as their teacher, to invent lessons that would connect their understanding with new mathematical information, again using language and symbols with which the students themselves could test the legitimacy of mathematical assertions.

In each of these examples, I was testing the potential of a problem to engage students in the kind of activity that would reveal their assumptions about a particular piece of mathematics. The problems that were used served to mediate between what the students already knew and what I wanted them to learn. By having a means of finding out what they were thinking and the language they would use to describe their thinking, I could devise instruction that would enable them to extend that thinking into new, unfamiliar domains. The domains in which the problems were posed were safe enough for students to feel that they could assert and legitimate their own approaches to solving the problems because they were reasoning about familiar structural relationships. Students did not feel reluctant to engage with the problems, they were not worried about getting wrong answers, and they did not need to check the answers they did get with the teacher.[4] This meant that they could engage in arguments with one another and with their teacher, and rehearse the activity of doing mathematics.

Inventing Tools for Classroom Communication

A second teaching task involved in teaching mathematics for understanding, and one that immediately follows from choosing and posing problems, is finding language and symbols which students and teachers can use to enable them to talk about the same mathematical content. "Doing mathematics" is about finding ways to represent quantitative relationships: "Mathematics studies the representation of one structure by another, and much of the actual work of mathematics is to determine exactly what structure is preserved in that representation" (Kaput, 1987, p. 23). If teaching about mathematics is to be responsive to students' assumptions about underlying mathematical structures, it follows that both students and teachers need some way to say or show what they are thinking about essential structural relationships. Moreover, such expressions of structural relationships should be fully comprehensible to outsiders as well as to the teachers and students. Teachers need to talk to students about mathematics in a language that enables students to comprehend what the problem is that the teacher is posing, and whether the solution strategies proposed are legitimate. At the same time, students need a language to express their thoughts to their teacher in a way that the teacher, who is more steeped in mathematical conventions, can understand. The way language and symbols are understood in the classroom depends on the development of shared meaning structures, and shared expectations about both the terms and the form of discourse (Cazden, 1988; Mehan, 1979).[5] Neither students and teachers, nor mathematicians, can argue about their assertions unless they agree on common definitions for the terms they are using in relation to some referent with which all parties are familiar. For example, teaching students that the distributive law means $a(b + c) = ab + ac$ would probably enable them to plug in values for a, b, and c and find that the two sides of the equation are equivalent, but it would not enable them to question or assert arguments about why that must be true. This kind of teaching implies that the seat of intellectual authority will continue to lie outside of the learner, in the teacher or the book, this contradicts the notion that mathematical knowledge is warranted by the learner's own reasoning process. In contrast, if students and teacher talk about the distributive law using familiar referents, they will be able to make assertions about the structure of the domain in which that law pertains, prove them, and refute the ones that are untrue.

Constructivist psychologists have been struggling with the theoretical contradictions between assuming that a person can understand only the knowledge that he or she personally constructs and the reality of communication and culturally shared meaning (Cobb, 1988; Steffe, 1988; von Glasersfeld, 1988). Teaching, however, proceeds with the assumption that this contradiction can somehow be managed, since the teacher is responsible for students becoming educated in the shared meaning of their culture by learning to use tools, like language and mathematics, for communicating in the society in which they live. In Vygotskian psychology (1978) and in American social psychology (cf. Blumer, 1977; Mead, 1934), the contradiction between individual constructivism and communication disappears because thought is considered to be the product of mediation between the self and the "generalized other." This view fits with the idea that teachers are responsible for educating students in the tools of their culture, even though students construct their own knowledge. Both Mead and Vygotsky view the tools that have developed to enable communication in society as also enabling the development of individual thinking. They argue that increasingly higher levels of individual reasoning are supported by the use of tools that exist in the culture, and that it is through acquiring these tools (including language and symbols) that the individual is able to articulate the meaning of his or her own ideas and construct ever more sophisticated understanding (Pea, 1987; Renger, 1980).

In the mathematics lessons that I have been teaching, I assumed that understanding would be a product of this interaction of the individual and the culture — the culture of the classroom as well as the culture of mathematics. On the basis of this assumption, I have been experimenting with what Pea would call "cognitive technologies" to enhance the individual reasoning that students bring to their school work on mathematics. In Pea's interpretation of symbolic theory, cognitive technologies include

> all symbol systems, including writing systems, logics, mathematical notation systems, models, theories, film and other pictorial media, and now symbolic computer languages ... any medium that helps transcend the limitations of the mind (for example, attention to goals, short-term memory span) in thinking, learning, and problem-solving activities. (Pea, 1987, p. 91)

Conventional mathematical symbols and procedures can serve as such cognitive technologies once they are mastered. My goal as a teacher of students who had not yet mastered these conventions was to find systems of communication that could bridge between the technologies that students already knew how to use to enhance their thinking, namely ordinary language and drawing, and the technologies that are conventionally used in mathematical applications and theory building.

One example of such a tool is the stories and drawings I taught to represent the groupings that are entailed in multiplying large numbers (Lampert, 1986a, 1986b). These stories and drawings symbolized the operations in ways that were meaningful to students and adequate to the task of expressing important mathematical structures. At first, the students gave stories to go with multiplications, such as 12 jars with 4 butterflies in each jar to go with 12×4, and I made drawings on the board to illustrate their different ideas about how the jars could be grouped so that it would not be necessary to count all of the butterflies. The stories and drawings were a way for teacher and students to communicate about what kind of grouping "moves" were legitimate because they were about domains whose constraints were known to the students and they were representative of the mathematics I wanted them to learn. They were able to use drawings and stories as a symbol system

with which to argue, for example, that it is legitimate to figure out 28 × 65 by first finding 30 × 65, and subtracting
the product of 2 × 65 from that, or in a more conventional
vein, that you could find 4 × 76 by finding 4 × 70 and adding that to 4 × 6. Talk about what was legitimate in the
realm of stories and drawings was represented in numbers,
so that there was a reasoned basis for following the conventional procedure rather than doing it because "that's how
the teacher told me to do it."

A second experiment with a tool invented for classroom
communication about mathematics was teaching students
to use "pieces of pie" to represent decimal numbers, so that
they would have a way of supporting their assertions about
which of two numbers was larger (Lampert, 1990). In this
system, .39 was represented by "3 big pieces and 9 skinny
pieces" while .6 was "6 big pieces." By using this tool, students overcame their propensity to look at 39 and 6 as
quantities of equal-sized units, from which they would reasonably conclude that .39 was larger, and they had a way to
defend the idea that nine skinny pieces would not even be as
much a one big piece, even though there were more of them.
Students' drawings of pieces of pie enabled them to make
relationships among digits and place values, which they
had been unable to express using just digits with decimal
points. These kinds of pictures enabled me, as their
teacher, to talk about the trading relationship between
tenths and hundredths and thousandths, to support the
argument that .6 = .600, for example. The conventional
language of equivalent fractions was not familiar enough to
most of the students in the class to be used as the basis on
which to prove this equivalence, but when those fractions
were represented as pieces of pie, the evidence was such
that everyone could reason about the legitimacy of "adding
zeroes behind the decimal point" without changing the
value of the number. Students also used this cognitive tool
to speculate about the largest decimal number that was
less than one, and the smallest decimal that was greater
than zero. Using pieces of pie, they were able to tell me what
they were thinking about these profound mathematical is-

sues, and I was able to pose problems in a language that was meaningful to them.

Another exploration of this sort of tool for communication did not involve pictorial representations, but grew out of students' own way of speaking about relationships among higher and higher powers of a base number (Lampert, 1988). Students were able to think about generalizations in relationships among exponents without being distracted by the many digits in larger and larger powers by focusing only on "last digits." (For example, the last digit in 4^2 is 6, the last digit in 4^3 is 4, the last digit in 4^4 is 6 again, and in 4^5, it is 4 again; this alternation between 6 and 4 as last digits continues infinitely.) I was able to use this tool to engage a fifth grade class in speculating about, and then proving, that $7^2 \times 7^2$ would be 7^4, $7^4 \times 7^4$ would be 7^8, and so on. By constructing an isomorphism between the powers of seven and their last digits, students were able to argue about the structural basis for the laws of exponents as they apply to whole positive numbers in terms that made sense to them, and thus I was able to teach them about how mathematical structure of exponents is both related to and different from the mathematical structure of multiplication using the cognitive technology of "last digits."

All of these ways of communicating allowed the students to express their mathematics and the teacher to express her mathematics (Steffe, 1988) in the classroom community of discourse using languages with a common set of referents. Although each individual gives meaning to these referents independently, that meaning is shaped by the way the symbols are used in common activities. Part of teaching for understanding is giving symbols meaning in such a way as to enable the teacher to assess whether the way students understand something fits with his or her understanding, or the understanding that is common to the way these symbols are used in the discipline. In this way, communication in the classroom about mathematics can be a continual examination of the adequacy of the assumptions that are being made by teacher and students; this examination can occur if everyone has the sense that they are talking about the same thing.

A COMPARISON TO THE WISCONSIN MODEL AND SOME QUESTIONS

These experiments get students involved in mathematical discourse by posing problems that would incline them to reveal their assumptions about the structure of some piece of mathematics and instituting tools for classroom communication so that they and their teacher could argue about these assumptions. They seem to work; that is, one could observe that students had taken on a new way of treating their own knowledge. In conversation with the teacher, students explored assumptions, both verbally and in writing, at home and in class, and when examined individually, they could both defend and use the strategies they had learned for doing mathematics. These findings suggest that it is possible to develop and use a pedagogy based on mathematical epistemology in teaching mathematics in school, that is, it is possible for a fourth- or fifth-grade teacher to teach in ways that enable students to connect their assumptions about how mathematics works with the mathematical ideas that underlie the school curriculum and the conventions of the discipline. These findings provide some basis for asserting that such activity can occur in an ordinary school classroom, given the many constraints of that setting as it is now constituted. This raises questions about a considerable body of research on teaching which construes attending to students' individual ways of thinking as contradictory to the school's role as a public institution where learners interact with teachers in age-graded large groups (Berlak & Berlak, 1981; Cuban, 1984; Gracey, 1972; Jackson, 1968; McPherson, 1972; Metz, 1978; Sarason, 1971; Waller, 1932). A review of this literature by the author (Lampert, 1981) suggests that the sort of teaching that might follow from cognitive theories of mathematics learning (Carpenter & Fennema, 1988) is simply impossible to do in public school classrooms. But asserting that such teaching is possible also raises the question of whether or not it is feasible for such teaching to occur more broadly, and suggests questions about what sort of teacher skills and knowledge and institutional resources and reorganization are necessary to support it.

The Cognitively Guided Instruction project provides one set of answers to those questions, within the framework of teaching addition and subtraction in first grade. In this project, the researchers concluded that it is indeed possible for teachers to teach following principles of learning derived from cognitive theory and research (Carpenter et al, 1988). What enabled that teaching to occur? If the finding and posing of good problems, and the construction of tools to enable communication are thought of as problems that teachers need to solve in order to teach mathematics for understanding, then the way in which the CGI project has codified the findings of cognitive research on how children develop in their ability to do addition and subtraction of single digit numbers could be construed as a tool teachers use to solve those problems. In the CGI project, pedagogical knowledge is knowledge of the research findings of learning psychology. One of the questions facing researchers and policy makers, then, is whether similar tools based on similar bodies of psychological research are necessary to have this kind of teaching occur at other grade levels and in other topical areas.

In the CGI project, from which the Wisconsin Model is derived, first-grade students work on problems to be solved using addition and subtraction (Carpenter & Fennema, 1988). Using research knowledge about how children think about different types of problems, the CGI teachers listen and find out what their individual students understand about addition and subtraction to gain the particular knowledge they need to design appropriate instruction for each child. These teachers think about what they hear when they listen to students' solutions in terms of a codification of more and less sophisticated strategies for doing addition and subtraction problems derived from research, and they structure the classroom environment so that students will be encouraged to move toward increasingly sophisticated strategies: "CGI teachers found out what children knew about addition and subtraction by using the knowledge of problem types and solution strategies" (Fennema, Carpenter, & Peterson, 1990, p. 207). Some teachers used the map provided by the problem types to interact with individuals or to set problems for small groups to work on, while others used it to set an agenda that the class as a whole would follow (Fennema, Carpenter, & Peterson, 1990, p. 208). The problem types and solution strategies gave the teachers both a schema for choosing and posing problems, and a language for understanding what students said as they solved problems. Psychology, rather than mathematics, provided both the problems they would use to elicit students' thinking and the tools they would use to communicate with students.

Basing interaction on the problem types ensured that teachers and students would be speaking the same language and moving around in the same mathematical territory in relation to the operations of addition and subtraction. Because they were based on clinical research that established what children would do when posed certain kinds of problems, the problems were safe. They engaged students at a level wherein they could independently establish the reasonability of their results. The problems were also reliably productive, in the sense that they seemed to create an environment in which students would move along a developmental hierarchy that ended up at the place where the first-grade curriculum assumed they should be. The problem of designing interaction so that students develop in the direction of instructional goals was solved for CGI teachers by the research finding that even in the absence of instruction,

> children's solution strategies to addition and subtraction problems become increasingly abstract. Initially they solve simple problems by direct modeling; they move on first to increasingly

sophisticated counting strategies, to using derived facts and finally to recall of number facts.
(Fennema, Carpenter, & Peterson, 1990, p. 201)

The outcome of normal cognitive development is thus con-
gruent with the conventional expectations for what students ought to know by the time they complete first grade
(Carpenter & Moser, 1983). As first graders progress
through more and more sophisticated levels, they master
number facts and they can solve word problems with them,
having constructed a meaningful relationship between
symbolic and other strategies for solving such problems. So
the CGI teachers could assume that if they posed problems
of the type that had been used in the research, they would
be moving their students from the kind of mathematical
structures that were familiar to them before they came to
school (direct modeling) to the kind of mathematics teachers wanted to them to learn (derived facts and recall of number facts).

The knowledge that children's thinking about addition
and subtraction develops in this way "sets teachers free"
(Peterson, 1988, p. 35) from worrying about whether they
are fulfilling their public responsibilities for what children
are supposed to learn in the first grade. It means that the
teachers' thinking about what they are responsible for
teaching in mathematics does not need to be revised in order to accommodate Cognitively Guided Instruction. The
research informed them that children they taught would
develop the skills and knowledge they would be expected to
have in second grade, and when they engaged in CGI in
their classrooms, the research was confirmed. So the CGI
teachers could be satisfied that they were "covering the curriculum" (Peterson, 1988, p. 36).

Comparing CGI and the teaching I have done raises the
question of whether cognitive maps, like the one derived
from the addition and subtraction research, can substitute for mathematical maps as the structure for designing
teacher-student interaction and the basis for doing research that relates teaching and learning mathematics

with understanding in school. Nothing like the "problem types" for addition and subtraction exists for most of the upper elementary and secondary curriculum. The maps that are available to guide decisions about what sort of problems to pose and what sort of symbolic system to use to communicate with students about their mathematical ideas are derived from knowledge of mathematical structures, knowledge of the curriculum materials that are available for use with fourth and fifth graders, and knowledge of what is familiar to fourth and fifth graders. At this level, there is no evidence that students "naturally" develop toward appropriate instructional goals like being able to use a reasonable strategy for multiplying large numbers, or being able to explain how operating with exponents is different from multiplication. Neither is there evidence that students naturally develop a propensity to establish the validity of their knowledge on the basis of mathematical argument, rather than asking the teacher whether or not their answers are "right." In fact, there is considerable evidence to the contrary (Ball, 1988; National Assessment of Education Progress, 1988; Stodolsky, 1988).

Mathematical content like ordering decimal numbers or figuring rates and ratios encompasses and is joined in multiple ways to content in number, measurement, multiplication, division, and place value. Behr et al. (1983) refer to these as some of the "elementary but deep concepts" that make up the mathematical domain of rational numbers. Abstractions are built upon abstractions within these concepts, in ways that depend on the symbolic and computational tools the problem solver has at his or her disposal. Using mathematical reasoning to solve problems that involve ordering decimals, or using rates and ratios, connects these concepts in the context of the problem in addition to those concepts being connected in a web of structural relationships within the discipline. It is hard to imagine a simple hierarchy from less to more "mature" understandings in this kind of problem solving such as the one CGI relies on for helping teachers know how to move around in the domain of simple addition and subtraction. Cognitive re-

searchers in this area have continually encountered difficulties in trying to simplify this content into hierarchical
structures, and have not reached agreement even about the
boundaries of the domain (Hiebert & Behr, 1988). Given
these problems at the theoretical level, it is difficult to imagine a tool that would enable the teacher to know just what
sort of problem was "slightly harder," without the teacher
also having some knowledge of the mathematical structures themselves, and their multiple interconnections.

It is also difficult to imagine teachers posing problems
in the content domains that are encompassed by the upper
elementary mathematics curriculum without some appre-
ciation of the particular nature of mathematical solutions,
as opposed to other ways of thinking about problems (Russell, 1988). If students are given a problem like "How would
you share seven cookies among yourself and three friends?"
they might interpret the problem as one requiring quantitative reasoning, but they might also want to consider
which of their friends is feeling especially hungry, who likes
which kind of cookie, who has what for dessert after lunch,
and so on. "Mathematizing" the problem means putting
these qualitative considerations aside to make an abstract
model of the relationship between children and cookies.
One way of thinking about cognitive development is to assert that this approach is more mature, but it may also be
interpreted as simply different, and particular to Western
industrialized culture. (cf. Davis & Hersch, 1987) If knowledge about this difference between mathematical and non-
mathematical ways of judging the legitimacy of a solution
were not part of the teachers' repertoire, how would he or
she make decisions about responding to students' proposed solutions?

The fact that students are more "schooled" at the point
where topics like ratio and comparing decimal numbers begin to appear in the curriculum adds to the difficulty of producing and using the sort of tool that guided Cognitively
Guided Instruction in addition and subtraction. When students have been taught mathematics in school for four
years it is more difficult to find out how they think about

the content when they are solving a problem, because how they think is more mixed up with what they have learned to do. One needs to work to find problems that do not elicit rote responses, and in any response, one cannot easily separate the student's reasoning from his or her use of the tools learned from others. The goal of teaching at this level could even be construed as integrating these kinds of knowing into a smoothly functioning expertise (Nesher, 1986). For the teacher, attempting to separate the knowledge that children arrive at by reasoning from the knowledge they have acquired from previous instruction is difficult. This is because students come from so many different instructional backgrounds, including school instruction, parent and sibling instruction, and television.

If this interaction between the knowledge that students bring with them to the classroom and the acquisition of the mathematical tools of the culture is considered, content frameworks of the sort that guided the CGI research would need to take account of the relationship between mathematical knowledge acquired by reasoning at various levels of difficulty and the mathematical knowledge acquired from living and working in a society where people use disciplinary tools that have been developing over centuries to communicate and build new theories about quantitative relationships. Mathematical language and symbols, and conventions like writing numbers in base 10, are accepted as conventions by groups of people who wish to work together on solving problems (Pea, 1987). The reasoning that students do in the base-10 system is possible, in part because they have accepted a cultural convention; it is not equivalent to reasoning about the mathematical structure of number (Kaput, 1987). Other cultures have reasoned about number using different conventions, and used these conventions to develop sophisticated sciences and technological tools which were not available to cultures with the conventions that are familiar to us (for example, the Maya, who used a combination of base 5 and base 20 and invented a way of justifying the lunar and solar cycles to produce a calendar in these bases that was more accurate than any in

use in Europe in the same period of history (Morley & Brainerd, 1983)). When we think about what we want students
to learn about mathematical structures, it seems important to pay attention to these distinctions.

This distinction between reasoning about mathematical structures and using the tools that have developed as
part of our culture seems important as students move up
through the grades and are faced with learning about usable formulas in languages like algebra and Euclidean geometry, but it also pertains in first grade and has a great
deal to do with how we think teaching works to connect students' reasoning with mathematical conventions. For example, a CGI teacher was reported to pose the problem,
"When we went to the school forest yesterday, Juan collected 24 acorns and Betty collected 18 acorns. How many
acorns did they bring back to our class?" She then responded to students' solutions by pointing out the role of
groups of 10 in finding the sum of such large numbers
(Fennema, Carpenter, & Peterson, 1990, p. 216). What if
one of the students had figured out 24 + 18 by putting out
some blocks and noticing that what he or she had was 4
groups of 6 plus 3 groups of 6, and said the answer was 7
groups of 6, rather than 42, which is the conventional way
of saying 4 groups of 10 and 2 more? Should this kind of
alternative strategy be encouraged by the teacher, or only
those that use groupings based on ten? Both are reasonable and mathematically legitimate, but the groups-of-10 solution is the one we use most often in our culture. Both
might develop equally naturally if we did not have a language for counting built on a number base of 10 that is
learned by children from their parents. Breaking numbers
up by tens is a strategy that children invent because they
have been educated to do so, just as they are educated to
think of minutes in groups of 15, 30, and 60 (so that, for
example, 38 + 45 could be 30 + 30 = 1 and 8 + 15 = 23,
making a total of 1.23). When a teacher says, in the midst of
children's inventing strategies to add 24 acorns and 18
acorns, "Can anyone tell me how many tens are in 42?" she
is leading them to consider using a tool that members of our

culture use to communicate about quantitative relationships. It is not the only or necessarily the most reasonable
way to do so.

Because this cultural kind of knowledge is constructed
by the learner in communication with an adult who is
steeped in mathematical conventions, it puts the teacher in
a different kind of authority relationship with the learner,
and it means that the teacher needs to know something
more than how to get children to reason about quantitative
relationships. In terms of research, as Sinclair puts it,

> The difficulty of studying learning—and teaching
> —lies, in my view, in the fact that it demands the
> study of processes by which children come to
> know in a short time basic principles (in mathe-
> matics, but also in other scientific disciplines)
> which it took humanity thousands of years to
> construct. (1988, p. 1)

One key to addressing that difficulty is understanding what
knowledge should be represented in the learning environment (including what the teacher knows), analyzing what
the environment communicates to students about mathematics, and determining how these factors interact with
what students figure out for themselves.

How does a teacher decide when to "tell" students that it
might be helpful to think about something like "how many
tens are in 42?" And what other cultural tools might teachers want to tell their students about? And how can the telling be integrated into interactions that assume that students reason for themselves to decide what mathematics is
true? In the CGI project and in the research and development project on which I have reported here, posing problems which engage students in using their mathematical
knowledge is central to the act of teaching. Teachers who
pose problems are also telling students something about
what mathematics is and what mathematics they need to
know. If these problems are going to lead students in the direction of the mathematical richness of our culture, we
need to know more about how teachers might decide which

problems are appropriate, how the symbols and languages they decide to use in classroom communication about mathematics contribute to learning in the classroom, and how psychological and mathematical knowledge might contribute to those decisions.

These observations suggest that "pedagogical content knowledge" might not be the correct term to apply to what cognitive science can provide to guide teachers' decisions. Pedagogical content knowledge is knowledge for *teaching.* Knowledge about cognition is knowledge about *knowing* and perhaps about *learning.* Teachers need to have knowledge about knowing and learning if they are going to teach mathematics, but it may not be sufficient to guide that teaching. In our enthusiasm for what cognitive science can contribute to teachers' knowledge, we might be leaving out some other important things they also need to know. "Pedagogical knowledge" as it is defined by Carpenter and Fennema (1988, pp. 9–10) in relation to the findings of cognitive research may not capture all that teachers need to know about content. As Shulman originally used the term, pedagogical content knowledge was meant to be a subset of what teachers need to know about content, and a subset of what teachers need to know about pedagogy. The kinds of content frameworks generated by cognitive science are certainly helpful in figuring out how what learners bring connects with what we want them to learn, but they are limited portrayals of the nature of mathematical knowledge. The strength of the approach taken by the CGI project is that it demands less of teachers in the way of subject matter knowledge. It makes correspondingly heavier demands on researchers to develop frameworks that teachers can use as tools in posing problems and communicating with learners. The approach I have taken, in contrast, makes heavy and perhaps unrealistic demands on teachers. In order to choose and pose appropriate problems and to institute appropriate tools for arguing about mathematical assumptions in the classroom using mathematics as the starting point, teachers would need to know a great deal more about both content and discourse in the discipline. But they would gain in the capacity to respond more flexibly to students' thinking by moving around in a deeper and broader mathematical territory.

NOTES TO CHAPTER 5

1. The work I will review here is described more fully in Lampert, 1985b, 1986a, 1986b, 1988, and 1989.

2. This problem was found in Cook, 1982, and adaptions were made of it over the course of several lessons.

3. The source of this problem was a conversation with another teacher.

4. See Schoenfeld, 1985 and Cooney, 1987 for a discussion of the propensity that students have for these kinds of responses to problem solving activities in the context of school lessons.

5. These shared assumptions need not support what a disciplinary expert would identify as understanding. They can just as well support the legitimacy of rote memorization or no learning at all.

REFERENCES

Balacheff, N. (1987). Procèsses de preuve et situations de validation. *Educational Studies in Mathematics, 18,* 147–176.
Ball, D. L. (1988). *Knowledge and reasoning in mathematical pedagogy: Examining what prospective teachers bring to teacher education: Teachers' subject matter knowledge.* Unpublished doctoral dissertation, Michigan State University.
———. (in press). Research on teaching mathematics: Making subject matter knowledge part of the equation. In J. Brophy (Ed.), *Advances in research on teaching* (Vol. 2). Greenwich, CT: JAI Press.
Behr, M., Lesh, R., Post, T., & Silver, E. (1983). Rational number concepts. In R. Lesh & M. Landau (Eds.), *Acquisition of mathematics concepts and processes.* Orlando, FL: Academic Press.
Berger, P. L., & Luckmann, T. (1967). *The social construction of reality: A treatise in the sociology of knowledge.* New York: Anchor.

Berlak, A., & Berlak, H. (1981). *Dilemmas of schooling: Teaching and social change.* New York: Methuen.

Blumer, H. (1977). Sociological implications of the thought of George Herbert Mead. In B. R. Cosin, et al. (Eds.), *School and society: A sociological reader* (pp. 16–22). London: Routledge & Kegan Paul.

Bruner, J. (1986). *Actual minds, Possible worlds.* Cambridge: Harvard University Press.

Carnegie Forum on Education and the Economy. (1986). *A nation prepared: Teachers for the 21st century.* New York: Carnegie Forum.

Carpenter, T. P., & Fennema, E. (1988). *Research and cognitively guided instruction.* Madison, WI: National Center for Research in Mathematical Sciences Education.

Carpenter, T. P., Fennema, E., Peterson, P. L., Chiang, C. P., & Loef, M. (April, 1988). *Using knowledge of children's mathematical thinking in classroom teaching: An experimental study.* Paper presented at the American Educational Research Association Annual Meeting, New Orleans, LA.

Carpenter, T. P., & Moser, J. M. (1983). The acquisition of addition and subtraction concepts. In R. Lesh & M. Landau (Eds.), *Acquisition of mathematics concepts and processes* (pp. 7–44). NY: Academic Press.

Cazden, C. B. (1988). *Classroom discourse: The language of teaching and learning.* Portsmouth, NJ: Heinemann.

Cobb, P. (1988, April). *Experiential, cognitive, and anthropological perspectives in mathematics education.* Paper presented at the American Educational Research Association Annual Meeting, New Orleans.

Cook, M. (1982). *Think about it! Mathematics problems of the day.* Palo Alto, CA: Creative Publications.

Cooney, T. J. (1987, October). *The issue of reform: What have we learned from yesteryear?* Paper presented at the Mathematical Science Education Board and the Center for Academic Interinstitutional Program Conference, UCLA.

Cuban, L. (1984). Policy and research dilemmas in the teaching of reasoning: Unplanned designs. *Review of Educational Research, 54*(4), 655–681.

Davis, P. J., & Hersh, R. (1981). *The mathematical experience.* Boston: Houghton Mifflin.

———. (1987). *Descartes dream: The world according to math-*

ematics. New York: Harcourt, Brace, Jovanovich.

Fennema, E., Carpenter, T. P., & Peterson, P. L. (1989). Learning mathematics with understanding. In J. Brophy (Ed.), *Advances in research on teaching* (Vol. 1, pp. 195–221). Greenwich, CT: JAI Press.

Florio, S., & Clark, C. (1984). *Written literacy forum: Combining research and practice* (Research Series No. 138). East Lansing: Michigan State University, Institute for Research on Teacher Education.

Frederikson, N. (1984). Implications of cognitive theory for instruction in problem solving. *Review of Educational Research, 54,* 363–407.

Geertz, C. (1973). *The interpretation of cultures.* New York: Basic Books.

Gelman, R. (1986). Toward an understanding-based theory of mathematics learning and instruction, or, in praise of Lampert on teaching multiplication. *Cognition and Instruction, 3,* 349–356.

Ginsburg, H. P., & Yamamoto, T. (1986). Understanding, motivation, and teaching: Comment on Lampert's "Knowing, doing, and teaching multiplication." *Cognition and Instruction, 3,* 357–370.

Gracey, H. L. (1972). *Curriculum or craftsmanship: Elementary school teachers in a bureaucratic setting.* Chicago: University of Chicago Press.

Green, T. F. (1971). *The activities of teaching.* NY: McGraw-Hill.

Greeno, J. G. (1986). Collaborative teaching and making sense of symbols: Comments on Lampert's "Knowing, doing, and teaching multiplication." *Cognition and Instruction, 3,* 343–348.

Greeno, J., Riley, M., & Gelman, R. (1984). Conceptual competence and children's counting. *Cognitive Psychology, 16,* 94–134.

Hammersly, M. (1979). Towards a model of teacher activity. In J. Eggleston (Ed.), *Teaching decision-making in the classroom: A collection of papers* (pp. 181–192). London: Routledge & Kegan Paul.

Hawkins, D. (1974). I, thou, and it. In D. Hawkins (Ed.), *The informed vision: Essays on learning and human nature* (pp. 48–62). New York: Agathon Press.

Hiebert, J. & Behr, M. (1988). Introduction: Capturing the major themes. In J. Hiebert & M. Behr (Eds.), *Number concepts and operations in the middle grades* (pp. 1 – 18). Hillsdale, NJ: Lawrence Erlbaum Associates.

Holmes Group, Inc. (1986). *Tomorrow's teachers.* East Lansing, MI: Holmes Group, Inc.

Jackson, P. W. (1968). *Life in classrooms.* New York: Holt, Rinehart & Winston.

Kaput, J. (1987). Representation systems and mathematics. In C. Janvier (Ed.), *Problems of representation in the teaching and learning of mathematics* (pp. 19–26). Hillsdale, NJ: Lawrence Erlbaum Associates.

Kilpatrick, J. (1987). Problem formulating: Where do good problems come from? In A. H. Schoenfeld (Ed.), *Cognitive Science and mathematics education* (pp. 123 – 148). Hillsdale, NJ: Lawrence Erlbaum Associates.

Kramer, E. E. (1970). *The nature and growth of modern mathematics.* Princeton, NJ: Princeton University Press.

Lakatos, I. (1976). *Proofs and refutations: The logic of mathematical discovery.* New York: Cambridge University Press.

Lampert, M. (1981). *How teachers manage to teach: Perspectives on the unsolvable dilemmas in teaching practice.* Unpublished doctoral dissertation, Harvard Graduate School of Education.

———. (1985a). How do teachers manage to teach? *Harvard Educational Review, 55,* 178–194.

———. (1985b). Mathematics learning in context: The Voyage of the Mimi. *Journal of Mathematical Behavior, 4,* 157–168.

———. (1986a). Knowing, doing, and teaching multiplication. *Cognition and Instruction, 3,* 305–342.

———. (1986b). Teaching multiplication. *Journal of Mathematical Behavior, 5,* 241–280.

———. (1988, November). *The teacher's role in reinventing the meaning of mathematical knowing in the classroom.* Paper presented for Psychology of Mathematics Education-North America Conference, DeKalb, Illinois.

———. (1989). Choosing and using mathematical tools in classroom discourse. In J. Brophy (Ed.), *Advances in research on teaching* (Vol. 1) (pp. 223–264). Greenwich, CT: JAI Press.

Lortie, D. (1975). *Schoolteacher: A sociological study.* Chicago: University of Chicago Press.

McPherson, G. (1972). *Small town teacher.* Cambridge: Harvard University Press.

Mead, G. H. (1934). *Mind, self, and society.* Chicago: University of Chicago Press.

Mehan, H. (1979). *Learning lessons.* Cambridge: Harvard University Press.

Metz, M. H. (1978). *Classrooms and corridors: The crisis of authority in desegregated secondary schools.* Berkeley and Los Angeles: University of California Press.

Morley, S. G., & Brainerd, G. W. (1983). *The ancient Maya.* Stanford, CA: Stanford University Press.

National Assessment of Educational Progress. (1988). *The mathematics report card: Are we measuring up?* Princeton, NJ: Educational Testing Service.

Nesher, P. (1986). Are mathematical understanding and algorithmic performance related? *For the Learning of Mathematics, 6*(3), 2–9.

Pea, R. D. (1987). Cognitive technologies for mathematics education. In A. H. Schoenfeld (Ed.), *Cognitive Science and mathematics education* (pp. 89–122). Hillsdale, NJ: Lawrence Erlbaum Associates.

Peterson, P. L. (1988, April). *New roles and classroom practice.* Paper presented at the Annual Meeting of the American Educational Research Association, New Orleans, LA.

Polya, G. (1954). *Induction and analogy in mathematics.* Princeton, NJ: Princeton University Press.

Renger, P. (1980). George Herbert Mead's contribution to the philosophy of American education. *Educational Theory, 30,* 115–133.

Russell, S. J. (1988, July). *Issues in training teachers to teach statistics in the elementary school: A world of uncertainty.* Paper prepared for presentation at the International Statistics Institute Roundtable Conference, Rakeve, Hungary.

Sarason, S. (1971). *The culture of the school and the problem of change.* New York: Allyn and Bacon.

Scheffler, I. (1965). *Conditions of knowledge.* Chicago: The University of Chicago Press.

Schoenfeld, A. H. (1985). Metacognitive and epistemological issues in mathematical understanding. In E. A. Silver (Ed.), *Teaching and learning mathematical problem solving: Multiple research perspectives* (pp. 361–379). Hillsdale, NJ: Lawrence Erlbaum Associates.

Scribner, S. (1984). Studying working intelligence. In B. Rogoff & J. Lave (Eds.), *Everyday cognition: Its development in social context* (pp. 9–40). Cambridge: Harvard University Press.

Shulman, L. (1988). *Learning for teaching.* Paper prepared for Tomorrow's Schools Seminar, Holmes Group, East Lansing, MI.

Sinclair, H. (1988, July). *Learning: The interactive re-creation of knowledge.* Paper prepared for the International Congress on Mathematics Education, Budapest, Hungary.

Steffe, L. P. (1988, July). *Principles of mathematics curriculum design: A constructivist perspective.* Paper presented at the International Congress of Mathematics Education, Budapest, Hungary.

Stodolsky, S. S. (1988). *The subject matters: Classroom activity in math and social studies.* Chicago: University of Chicago Press.

Taylor, C. (1979). Interpretation and the sciences of man. In P. Rabinow & W. M. Sullivan (Eds.), *Interpretive social science: A reader* (pp. 33 – 81). Berkeley and Los Angeles: University of California Press.

von Glasersfeld, E. (1988, July). *Environment and communication.* Paper delivered at the International Congress on Mathematics Education, Budapest, Hungary.

Vygotsky, L. S. (1978). *Mind in society: The development of the higher psychological processes.* Cambridge: Harvard University Press.

Waller, W. (1932). *The sociology of teaching.* New York: John Wiley & Sons.

6

Methodologies for Studying Learning to Inform Teaching

James Hiebert and Diana Wearne

We view this chapter as an opportunity to increase the dialogue among those involved in research on learning and teaching mathematics. We have taken seriously the invitation of the Wisconsin group to consider the paper as a basis for communication and discussion rather than as a report of an individual research program. Consequently, we focus on issues that provide points of contact between our work and that of others, especially the current work at Wisconsin.

The issues we have chosen emerge from paradigmatic and methodological questions. Because the research domain that bridges the gap between learning and teaching is not yet well-developed, it seems appropriate to focus some of the discussion on issues that are relatively fundamental. At this point in our collective research history, questions of which research paradigms are most appropriate and which methodologies are both paradigmatically consistent and productive are important questions to consider.

We begin the chapter by noting a significant difference between the goal of our current work and the Cognitively Guided Instruction (CGI) project at Wisconsin. Although the difference appears at first glance to result from a difference in research paradigms, we eventually attribute it to a difference in the maturity of the learning research in different mathematical topic domains. We also suggest a distinction between models of research on teaching and models of instructional improvement. We then elaborate some aspects of a methodology that we believe is useful for studying learning in complex mathematical domains that are just beginning to be examined—in our case, decimal fractions. The aim is to provide information on learning that is especially useful for both studying and improving teaching. Along the way, we take detours to identify similarities and differences between our work and other related projects and to raise questions that might guide further work in this general field of research.

CONTRASTING GOALS AND PARADIGMS OF RESEARCH

It could be argued that the research in mathematics learning and in mathematics teaching have remained "two disciplines of scientific inquiry" (Romberg & Carpenter, 1986), because research in one domain has different goals than research in the other. The goal of our work over the past few years has been to understand how students think as they work with decimal fractions and to describe the cognitive processes that students acquire to solve decimal problems during specially designed instructional units. Our primary interest is how students *learn* decimals; the instruction we employ is specific and prescriptive.

In contrast, a primary goal of the CGI project is to understand how teachers' knowledge and beliefs influence the design and implementation of instruction. A basic premise of their approach is that instruction is not improved by prescribing particular forms of instruction but rather by "helping teachers make informed decisions" (Carpenter & Fennema, 1988, p. 12). Teachers are viewed as critical mediators of the instructional process. This means that whether or not new instructional materials and approaches reach the students depends on teachers' decisions. Therefore, handing teachers a completely specified instructional unit on decimal fractions is rejected as a useful way to improve instruction on decimals.

Clearly, the thrust of our work differs from the work at Wisconsin. Do we fall into different disciplines of scientific inquiry? Are we working within different paradigms? We believe that the answers to these questions are important because they may shed some light on the relationship between research on learning and on teaching and may contribute to conceptualizing paradigms that bridge the gap.

The CGI model can be viewed as a model for studying teaching and as a model for improving teaching. As a model for studying teaching, the focus is on examining the ways in which teachers use knowledge of students' learning to plan and implement instruction. As a model for improving teaching, the focus is on documenting an increase in students' learning and understanding that coincides with teachers' acquisition of knowledge about students' learning. The two models are not mutually exclusive but they do have different goals. The distinction between the models is useful for examining the relationship between research on learning and teaching in general and the relationship between our work and the Wisconsin work (CGI) in particular.

Consider first the CGI model as a model for improving instruction. We suggest that, in this case, the current work at Wisconsin is best interpreted as a component of a rich chain of inquiry that began with some basic research on children's learning. The CGI approach should be interpreted as a "model" only within this larger context. In other words, it is the chain of inquiry that serves as a model for improving instruction rather than the CGI work taken alone.

It is useful to trace back to the roots of the current work at Wisconsin. The chain of inquiry began with descriptions of children's thinking in simple addition and subtraction situations and with accompanying analyses of the content domain (for example, Carpenter, Hiebert, & Moser, 1981; Fuson, 1982; Lindvall & Ibarra, 1980; Nesher, Greeno, & Riley, 1982; Steffe, Thompson, & Richards, 1982). The precision and richness of the descriptions were increased by the development of theoretical models of children's thinking (Briars & Larkin, 1984; Riley, Greeno, & Heller, 1983). Attention then shifted to documenting changes in children's thinking as they became increasingly competent in solving addition and subtraction problems

(Carpenter & Moser, 1984). Finally, and immediately preceding the CGI project, research focused on the responses
of students to instruction that was specially designed to
promote certain competencies in addition and subtraction
(Carpenter, Moser, & Bebout, 1988). Many studies at each
stage, in addition to the few cited here, contributed to the
wealth of knowledge of children's learning of addition and
subtraction.

It seems to us that the uncommon success of the CGI
project in influencing instruction rests squarely on the extensive knowledge of children's learning generated by the
preceding work. Indeed, we conjecture that such extensive
knowledge in specific domains is a prerequisite for the success of a program that assumes that significant changes in
instruction are produced by providing teachers with information rather than prescribing instruction (Carpenter &
Fennema, 1988). We believe it is a prerequisite because it is
specific knowledge of children's learning that constitutes
the information provided to the teachers. The model for improving instruction rests upon sharing such knowledge
with the teachers. The recent reports of the project (Carpenter et al., 1988; Peterson et al., 1989) demonstrate the
extent to which this knowledge is used in every aspect of the
work, from assessment measures of teachers and students,
to teacher training, to observations of classrooms.

It seems to us inappropriate to interpret CGI as a model
for improving instruction outside of the context in which it
developed, apart from the larger research program of which
it is the most recent link. In topic domains (for example,
decimals, fractions, algebra) where learning research is
just beginning to map the terrain, the CGI model may not
work — yet. Even in topic areas that appear relatively early
in the school curriculum, such as multiplication and division of whole numbers and the introduction of fractions
and decimals, the subject matter becomes extremely complex and the processes involved in learning it are just beginning to be understood (Hiebert & Behr, 1988). At this point
we simply do not have enough information, at a sufficient
level of detail, to share with teachers.

Another way to argue for the importance of detailed information on students' learning before implementing the CGI approach as a way to improve instruction is by analogy. If less is known about the relationships between the content, the tasks, and the learning experience, fewer alternatives for structuring beneficial learning experiences can be described. If less of the map has been filled in, only one route to the goal may be known. The traveler is told exactly what route to follow. But if the map is relatively complete, the traveler can be informed of all the relevant features of the map, and the traveler can choose the route.

An important parenthetical note is that, although a rich body of knowledge on children's learning is *necessary* for the CGI approach to improve instruction, it probably is not *sufficient*. Other chains of inquiry, on teachers' knowledge and beliefs and how these influence instruction (for example, Leinhardt & Smith, 1985; Putnam, 1987; Schoenfeld, 1988; Shulman, 1986, 1987; Thompson, 1984), certainly contributed critical components to the CGI design. Particular evidence of this work is seen in the respect with which teachers are viewed as central decision makers in the instructional process. But we will not focus our attention on these connections. Our primary interest is the essential connection between the earlier work on children's learning and the assumptions on which CGI is based.

Consider now the CGI approach as a research model, as a model for studying teaching. In this case, the relationship between the CGI work and prior research on learning changes. As a research enterprise, the CGI approach is capable of serving as a model for studying teaching regardless of the level of information currently available on students' learning. The critical assumptions of the model have to do with how teachers use information about students to teach them. The critical feature of the work generated by the model is the *documentation* of how teachers use the information they are provided. Teachers' knowledge of students may be built from rich, detailed information, as for addition and subtraction, or from sketchy, imprecise information, as (currently) for multiplication and division. As long as the knowledge that teachers acquire and the way they use their knowledge is documented, we can learn about teaching and about the relationships between children's learning and teaching. Our understanding of how teachers use information on students' learning probably will grow with an increase in the richness of the information we can provide. But, for research purposes, detailed, extensive information is not necessary.

One final observation can be made about the relationship between learning and teaching in the CGI approach. As noted earlier, a critical assumption in the CGI research model is that the teacher is a decision maker. It is worth examining the CGI view of the teacher a little further because it reveals another link between learning and teaching.

The CGI model used to study teaching has an interesting parallel with a relatively recent view of learning. There has been a growing consensus in learning research that it is often more useful to describe children's intellectual competencies than to list their deficiencies. However, there remains a nagging dilemma: describing the competencies does not make the deficiencies go away. And the expert-novice studies illustrate how serious some of the deficiencies are. There are many potential ways to resolve the dilemma. Most of them involve studying changes in competencies rather than providing static descriptions of competencies or deficiencies. A perspective that is being used productively in learning research is one in which the learner is viewed as someone with important beginning competencies and as someone who is capable of extending or changing these competencies in desirable ways. Studying learning becomes studying the processes of change, under carefully described conditions, from currently useful competencies to better competencies.

In many ways, the CGI project is studying teaching in exactly this way. The investigators have avoided the dilemma of choosing between descriptions of competencies or deficiencies by focusing on changes in competencies. Teachers are viewed as learners with many useful initial competencies but with some deficiencies as well. Teachers

arc viewed as learners who can use information and experiences to extend and change their competencies in desirable ways, in ways that will eliminate or overcome their deficiencies.

To summarize, the CGI work might be viewed as an approach to improve teaching and as an approach to study
teaching. In the first case it should be interpreted within
the context of the prior research on learning. Furthermore,
its usefulness in other topic domains may depend on as-
sembling more information on students' learning. In the
second case it can serve, by itself, as a model for conducting
research on teaching. The level of information on students'
learning is not as crucial here so the model might be successfully employed now in other topic domains.

In either case, however, our position is that more information is needed on students' learning. In contrast to Romberg and Carpenter (1986), who suggest that much is
known about students' learning but less is known about
how to apply this knowledge to problems of instruction, we
believe not enough is known about learning in most mathematical domains to inform teaching. In these domains, we
believe that research on learning is a top priority. But we
also believe that some approaches to studying learning will
be more helpful than others in providing the kind of information a CGI model can use. In the remainder of the paper,
we describe a model for studying learning that has an eye
on instructional applications.

STUDYING LEARNING TO INFORM TEACHING

It is probably apparent by this time that we consider information on students' learning in specific domains to be essential. This is not to deny the importance of several do-
main-independent features of learning. For example, it is
generally agreed that students are active participants in
constructing their own knowledge rather than passive re-
cipients of information. It is also generally agreed that
learning mathematics involves a complex interaction of
conceptual and procedural knowledge rather than the ac-

quisition of one or the other. Although such insights about learning are significant, it seems that they are too general to impact instruction on their own. These insights need to be accompanied by detailed descriptions of what they mean in specific topic domains. In other words, these general features of learning, although significant and powerful, are perhaps more useful for interpreting domain-specific learning processes than for influencing instruction directly.

The question, then, is how do we investigate domain-specific learning to generate information that can be applied to instructional practice, perhaps using a CGI approach to both study and improve teaching. There are a number of methodologies that could be offered as productive ways to investigate learning. One kind of methodology, for example, is aimed toward uncovering the developmental precursors of competencies in a domain and then designing instruction to promote the development of these precursors, especially in populations where they are absent (Case, 1985, Chap. 18). Another kind of methodology focuses on the responses of subjects to various forms of instructional intervention (Belmont & Butterfield, 1977). The goal is to describe changes over instruction in subjects' processes for performing tasks. The two kinds of methodologies are not incompatible. In fact, we use the second as a backdrop for the methodological framework presented below, and much of the first to think about several components of the framework.

A Methodology for Studying Learning to Inform Teaching

In an earlier paper (Hiebert & Wearne, 1988), we outlined the primary ingredients in the methodology to be discussed here. We presented the methodology, based on the framework of Belmont and Butterfield (1977), as a way to bridge the gap between research on learning and research on teaching. It seems to us now that the methodology is better viewed as an approach for studying learning that fits into a larger chain of inquiry moving from research on learning to research on applying knowledge of learning to instruction. We will not repeat our comments from the earlier paper but will rather elaborate on certain aspects that seem especially likely to make contact with other work presented in this volume.

Briefly, the methodology involves (1) selecting the content domain and defining it clearly; (2) identifying the cognitive processes that are critical for successful performance in the domain; (3) designing instruction to promote the acquisition and use of the key processes; and (4) examining the relationship between instruction and cognitive change and assessing the extent of cognitive change. The first component reaffirms our view that it is essential to study learning in specific contexts. We will not discuss this component further but rather will focus attention on the remaining three components.

Identifying key cognitive processes. The most critical component of the methodology is the identification and description of cognitive processes that lead to competence in a domain. These processes become the "content" of the instructional intervention, and the assessment measures trace the acquisition and use of the processes. So the usefulness of the information provided by the research depends on the identification of appropriate processes.

Several different approaches have been used to identify the key cognitive processes in a domain. One approach analyzes the solution strategies and thoughts of experts as they solve problems. The cognitive processes uncovered through such analyses, especially when contrasted with those of novices, are usually thought to capture at least some of what it means to be competent in a domain. A second approach traces the development of "natural" strategies for solving problems in a domain. Learning research in early addition and subtraction found counting and the semantic interpretation of word problems to be two such strategies. Information obtained by documenting the details of these naturally emerging strategies turned out to be extremely useful for informing instruction (Carpenter et al., 1988; Peterson et al., 1989). A third approach utilizes task analyses and describes processes that could be used to perform the tasks. Subject matter specialists are helpful here because the processes identified should show some connection with processes that are used to deal with previously encountered content and should put the students in a good position to deal with future content. A range of alternate processes, rather than a single process, is likely to be identified.

It is not yet clear which approach, or what combination of approaches, might be most useful for identifying key cognitive processes in complex mathematical domains. However, some recent work on this problem in middle school mathematics (Hiebert & Behr, 1988) is beginning to converge toward some common themes. Using a variety of approaches, a number of investigators suggest that key cognitive processes can be identified, such as the construction of composite units (Steffe, 1988) and partitioning strategies (Kieren, 1988). These kinds of processes, along with others, might be thought of as theorems-in-action (Vergnaud, 1988) or as central conceptual structures (Case & Sandieson, 1988). What is important is that there seems to be a relatively small set of key processes that emerge early at an intuitive level and that contain the seeds of many of the more powerful formal methods that are taught later. Identifying them early and encouraging their development during instruction may place students in a good position to deal with the topics of middle school mathematics, such as multiplicative word problems (Nesher, 1988) and ratio and proportion (Hart, 1988; Lesh, Post, & Behr, 1988).

As work continues in the identification of key cognitive processes, we need to build more explicit models of the kinds of processes that generate success and competence in the long run. In other words, we need to build more explicit models of the cognitive processes that students *should* use in particular content domains. Specific features of useful processes may differ from domain to domain, but some general characteristics apply across domains. It is at this point that some of the more general findings from research on learning become useful.

One characteristic of all key processes, regardless of content, is that students can make them their own. Key processes need to be accessible to students. They need to have a character that permits a student to actively engage in connecting them to other things the student already knows. Students must be able to link them into their growing web of conceptual knowledge (Hiebert & Lefevre, 1986). If students invent the processes, such connections are almost assured. But key processes need not be invented or self-constructed. They can be presented through instruction. The crucial thing is that students take possession of the processes by hooking the processes into knowledge that already has meaning for them (cf. Cobb, 1988).

A second characteristic of all key processes is that they possess features of higher order thinking (Resnick, 1987). This means that key processes should involve some reflection, some recursion on themselves (Hofstadter, 1979; Kilpatrick, 1985). They should involve the construction of meaning and should support the general goal of making sense of situations. They should not be algorithmic or heavily prescriptive. The kinds of processes described earlier display these features. The semantic analyses of addition and subtraction word problems used by younger children and the theorems-in-action described by Vergnaud (1988) or the central conceptual structures described by Case and Sandieson (1988) for middle school students, all possess some salient features of higher order thinking. It is crucial to note that higher order thinking is not something that enters late in the development of competence and expertise but rather can and should be present, in some form, from the beginning (Resnick, 1987).

A third characteristic of key cognitive processes is that they transfer to novel contexts. It is simply impossible to become competent in mathematics if a different strategy or skill must be acquired to solve each kind of problem. There are too many different problems. Key cognitive processes are not so narrow and problem specific. They are at an appropriate level of generality so that they are useful in a variety of different contexts. But identifying an "appropriate" level is not an easy task. The dilemma is this: generalizable, content-free problem-solving heuristics are rather weak when applied to specific tasks. The heuristics carry little knowledge about any particular task and cannot, by themselves, bring to bear specific procedures that enable the task to be solved. On the other hand, specific procedures, that are very powerful on a small set of tasks, do not transfer well. They are connected too tightly to surface features of specific contexts.

A resolution of the dilemma may require a combination of the research approaches identified earlier: comparisons of expert and novice processes, identification of natural processes, and subject matter analyses. Progress is being made in identifying appropriate level processes in a number of topic areas in middle school mathematics (Hiebert & Behr, 1988). Progress is also being made in domains that cut across traditional curriculum topics. For example, cognitive processes involved in representing mathematical situations and in operating on these representations is receiving a great deal of attention (Davis, 1984; Goldin, 1987; Hiebert, 1988; Kaput, 1987; Lesh, Post, & Behr, 1987; Mason, 1987). The processes involved in constructing meaning for written mathematical symbols are now being described at a level of specificity that is bringing them within the methodological arena of key cognitive processes. That is, it is possible to study the acquisition of such processes under controlled instructional conditions (Wearne & Hiebert, 1988; Wearne, 1988).

To summarize, a critical component of the methodology we advocate for studying learning to inform teaching is the identification of key cognitive processes. The processes should capture the essence of competence in a particular mathematical domain. More specifically, the processes should be understood by students in an intellectually personal way, the processes should involve higher order thinking throughout their development, and they should be defined at a strategic level that makes them useful for solving specific problems on the one hand, but allows them to generalize to a variety of problems on the other. Such processes

are well-described in topic areas that have been heavily re-
searched, such as addition and subtraction, and are beginning to be identified in areas that have received recent attention, such as fractions and decimals. Once the
processes are identified, the methodology suggests studying students' acquisition of the processes during instruction. Of course, the information gained from the instructional intervention may help to refine the description of the
key processes. So the actual research program may include
several cycles of identifying processes and designing instruction to support their acquisition. The processes will
inform teaching, because they will make up the core information about students' learning that teachers can use.

Designing and implementing instructional intervention.
The primary goal of the methodology is to generate information on the relationships between acquiring key cognitive processes in a domain and instructional events that
support or hinder such acquisitions. To achieve the goal,
the instruction must be specifiable. This feature is necessary to trace the effects of instruction on the acquisition of
cognitive processes. If the instruction includes instructional strategies or episodes that cannot be described in detail, then one loses the hope of connecting the acquisition
of processes with instruction in any meaningful way.

Instruction has a much different meaning here than it
does in the CGI model or in other research on teaching. Instruction is used in the service of studying learning. It is
designed with an unusual degree of precision and implemented according to carefully prescribed guidelines. The
instruction might be carried out with a small group of students or with an entire class. In fact, there are some benefits in beginning with a small group for which instructional conditions can be controlled, and then moving to full
classroom settings that afford greater ecological validity.
The goal of designing and implementing instruction is not
to recommend any single instruction unit for importation
into the classroom, but to understand how particular kinds
of instruction influence students' learning. Information on

students' learning of key processes under different instructional conditions is the kind of information that is essential in CGI-like projects.

In decimal fractions, we are beginning to document connections between the learning experiences provided through instruction and changes in the cognitive processes students use to perform tasks (Hiebert & Wearne, 1988; Wearne & Hiebert, 1988). For example, active engagement with materials that display quantitative relationships in a salient way (for example, Dienes blocks) and then juxtaposing these concrete representations of quantities with written representations leads some students to change the processes they use to deal with written problems. Students move from using syntactic processes that operate on the form of the written symbols to using processes that operate on the associated quantitative referents. Students begin to reason with "conceptual entities" (Greeno, 1983) that are represented by the symbols rather than with the symbols themselves. The important methodological point is that the change in processes can be linked with particular instructional events.

Even though the results are encouraging, the information is limited. The information certainly could be made available to teachers in a CGI study of how teachers use the information. But it is not of sufficient detail and richness that one should expect greatly improved instruction. In other words, more research on learning is needed before the information base is sufficiently broad and detailed to share with teachers using a CGI approach as a way to improve instruction.

Assessing the extent of cognitive change. Changes in cognitive processes are not all-or-none phenomena. Some changes are slight or fragile; the new process may contain only some of the desired characteristics or may be applied to an overly narrow range of problems. Other changes may be temporary; the new process may be acquired and used for a brief time and then may disappear.

In order to measure the nature of cognitive change and

the extent to which targeted cognitive processes are acquired and used by students, we have found it useful to administer two kinds of assessment tasks—direct measures and transfer measures. Direct measures assess students' performance and solution processes in the content and task domain of instruction. Instruction is designed to promote the use of key cognitive processes in a specific domain; the direct measures assess whether and how students use the processes on the instructed tasks. Because the key cognitive processes are sufficient for performing the tasks, one would expect to observe solution strategies that evidence the use of the key processes.

In contrast to direct measures, transfer measures are tasks that have not been included in the instructional activities. In many cases the tasks are new to students. Although the key cognitive processes are sufficient for performing them, students must engage in some additional mental work to apply the processes. The processes may need to be extended beyond the bounds of classroom discussion or they may need to be applied in the face of unfamiliar surface features of tasks. Spontaneous use of the cognitive processes in these novel contexts tells us something about the flexibility and robustness with which students acquire and deploy the processes (Greeno, Riley, & Gelman, 1984).

Because transfer is not an all-or-none phenomenon it is appropriate to measure the degree of transfer. We have found it useful to distinguish at least two levels of transfer —near transfer and far transfer. Although the boundaries between these are sometimes difficult to define operationally, we can distinguish between them in principle. Near transfer involves the use of the key processes on a task that shares some surface features with the instructed tasks. The processes are extended to cover these new cases, but the processes are applied in much the same way as they were during instruction. Because of this, it is unlikely that any new knowledge is generated internally through performing the tasks. Far transfer, on the other hand, involves the use of the key cognitive processes in entirely new contexts. Applying the processes in these contexts requires recognizing the processes as general ways of thinking about the content rather than as strategies for performing tasks. Reflecting on the cognitive processes in this way is likely to generate additional knowledge for the learner about the content domain.

Illustrations from our work with decimal fractions may help to clarify the notions of direct measures and near and far transfer measures. The instructional units that we have designed and implemented over the past few years have focused on assisting students in making connections between concrete referents (Dienes blocks) for decimal numbers and the standard written symbols, and then encouraging students to use these connections to develop procedures for adding and subtracting decimals (Wearne, 1988; Wearne & Hiebert, 1988). The instruction, which consists of eight to ten thirty-minute sessions, deals only with units, tenths, and hundredths. Examples of direct measures, after the unit is completed, include laying out a block display of 2.04 (given the large base-10 block as the unit) and adding 2.3 + .16. Students have engaged in performing and discussing these kinds of tasks during instruction. Examples of near transfer measures include laying out a block display of 1.253 (given the large base-10 block as the unit, and having available the large base-10 blocks, the flat base-10 blocks, the long base-10 blocks, the long base-5 blocks, and the small cubes), and adding .416 + .13. Because students have not worked with thousandths, they must use the key process of partitioning quantities by 10 on the first problem to select appropriate concrete referents for such values (of course they may not know the word thousandth) and they must use the key process of combining like quantities on the second problem to decide which digits to add together. Examples of far transfer measures include laying out a block display for 2.3564 (under the same conditions as previous tasks) and choosing the larger of .368 and .37. In the first case, students must recognize that the available blocks are inadequate and must apply the partitioning process to describe the creation of new blocks. In the second case, students must see that the connections they have established between written symbols and quantities can be used to solve entirely new problems. The notion of thinking about quantities rather than symbols must be seen as a notion that generalizes across specific classes of problems.

Transferability is an important attribute of key cognitive processes, but it is not the only one. An additional attribute discussed earlier is that key cognitive processes involve higher order thinking from the beginning. It is likely that the processes emerge initially at an intuitive level and gradually become more explicit and formal (Kieren, 1988; Vergnaud, 1988). Assessing this attribute of cognitive processes requires longitudinal work measured in years rather than days or weeks. There are very few examples of this kind of research in mathematics learning. But longitudinal work is needed to complete the picture in particular content domains and to provide teachers with useful information.

The methodology we have described is not appropriate to guide longitudinal research of the kind that is needed. With its emphasis on specificity and its up-close view of the teaching-learning "laboratory," it is most useful for studying immediate connections between learning and instruction. Belmont and Butterfield (1977) include the assessment of durability of cognitive change in their description and, although durability requires longitudinal assessment, we have something quite different in mind. The long-term effects of acquiring key cognitive processes involve much more than whether the processes are retained. The long-term effects of interest have to do with the way in which early acquisition of key processes influences later learning. We conclude the paper with a brief argument for longitudinal research in learning mathematics.

Longitudinal Research on Learning to Inform Teaching

A central question in mathematics education is how competence in mathematics develops over time. Most mathematics educators believe that if students acquire solid understandings of early concepts they will be in a better position to learn later concepts in a meaningful way. Conceptual understanding is believed to have a cumulative effect. The benefits extend beyond the immediate content in which understanding is acquired to later content that builds on the former. The belief probably derives partly from observations of the hierarchical nature of mathematics and partly from conceptions of how the mind works.

But we have little empirical data to inform our speculations. Perhaps the best example of a longitudinal project that reveals how early competencies influence later learning is the three-year study of Carpenter and Moser (1984). The intraindividual analyses provide a great deal of information on changes in children's competencies over time. But even here the information is limited by the relatively conventional instruction children received. It is likely that many of the children in the sample did not acquire key cognitive processes that underlie a meaningful transition to the written symbols of addition and subtraction (see, for example, Carpenter, Hiebert, & Moser, 1983). One wonders how early instruction of the kind reported by Carpenter, Moser, and Bebout (1988) would change the way in which children develop competencies several years down the road. The long-term teaching experiment of the Rational Number Project (Behr et al., 1984; Post et al., 1985) provides another kind of information on children's learning. In particular, the evidence reveals the extreme complexity of the simple-sounding topic of "fraction" and illustrates the corresponding difficulties students have in understanding it. Even though not all students in the project were entirely successful, it may be that these students are making more sense of the instruction they are currently receiving on fractions (and related topics). It may be that these students began the construction and acquisition of key cognitive processes and that the significant benefits of these acquisitions will emerge over time. The data on whole number subtraction presented by Hatano and Suga (1986) suggest that this is exactly what happens. The effects of acquiring key conceptual processes are more apparent later than sooner. But the entire collection of data on this question is still too limited to move us much beyond speculation.

Theoretical models and associated methodologies are needed to guide further work. One way of conceptualizing the issue is to consider the relationship between short-term and long-term change (Case, 1988). The methodology outlined in this paper is useful for studying short-term change. Although this represents progress over static descriptions of behavior, the ultimate question for those studying learning is how the short-term changes, perhaps induced by instructional intervention, influence learning in the long run. How do short-term changes in relatively local contexts contribute to broader changes across related domains? Do the same mechanisms of change operate in the short run as in the long run? Do students who acquire key cognitive processes in specific domains (for example, whole number multidigit addition and subtraction) extend these processes to encompass later content (for example, decimal addition and subtraction), or is there discontinuity between early and later processes? Information on these questions would be extremely useful to teachers in planning instruction. Certainly, teachers participating in CGI projects that focus on more advanced mathematical topics need more information than we can currently provide. We believe that the most useful information at this point will be obtained through costly, labor-intensive longitudinal work.

REFERENCES

Behr, M. J., Wachsmuth, I., Post, T. R., & Lesh, R. (1984). Order and equivalence of rational numbers: A clinical teaching experiment. *Journal for Research in Mathematics Education, 15,* 323–341.

Belmont, J. M., & Butterfield, E. C. (1977). The instructional approach to developmental cognitive research. In R. V. Kail, Jr. & J. W. Hagen (Eds.), *Perspectives on the development of memory and cognition* (pp. 437–481). Hillsdale, NJ: Lawrence Erlbaum Associates.

Briars, D. J., & Larkin, J. H. (1984). An integrated model of skill in solving elementary word problems. *Cognition and Instruction, 1,* 245–296.

Carpenter, T. P., & Fennema, E. (1988). *Research and cognitively guided instruction.* Madison, WI: National Center for Research in Mathematical Sciences Education.

Carpenter, T. P., Fennema, E., Peterson, P. L., & Carey, D. A. (1988). Teachers' pedagogical content knowledge of students' problem solving in elementary arithmetic. *Journal for Research in Mathematics Education, 19*(5), 385–401.

Carpenter, T. P., Hiebert, J., & Moser, J. M. (1981). Problem structure and first-grade children's initial solution processes for simple addition and subtraction problems. *Journal for Research in Mathematics Education, 12,* 27–39.

Carpenter, T. P., Hiebert, J., & Moser, J. M. (1983). The effect of instruction on children's solutions of addition and subtraction word problems. *Educational Studies in Mathematics, 14,* 35–72.

Carpenter, T. P., & Moser, J. M. (1984). The acquisition of addition and subtraction concepts in grades one through three. *Journal for Research in Mathematics Education, 15,* 179–202.

Carpenter, T. P., Moser, J. M., & Bebout, H. (1988). Representation of addition and subtraction word problems. *Journal for Research in Mathematics Education, 19*(4), 345–357.

Case, R. (1985). *Intellectual development: Birth to adulthood.* New York: Academic Press.

———. (1988). Summary comments: Developing a research agenda for mathematics in the middle grades. In M. Behr & J. Hiebert (Eds.), *Research agenda for mathematics education: Number concepts and operations in the middle grades* (pp. 265–270). Reston, VA: National Council of Teachers of Mathematics.

Case, R., & Sandieson, R. (1988). A developmental approach to the identification and teaching of central conceptual structures in mathematics and science in the middle grades. In J. Hiebert & M. Behr (Eds.), *Research agenda in mathematics education: Number concepts and operations in the middle grades* (pp. 236–250). Reston, VA: National Council of Teachers of Mathematics.

Cobb, P. (1988). The tension between theories of learning and instruction in mathematics education. *Educational Psychologist, 23*(2), 87–103.

Davis, R. B. (1984). *Learning mathematics: The cognitive science approach to mathematics education.* Norwood, NJ: Ablex.

Fuson, K. C. (1982). An analysis of the counting-on solution procedure in addition. In T. P. Carpenter, J. M. Moser, & T. A. Romberg (Eds.). *Addition and subtraction: A cognitive perspective* (pp. 68–81). Hillsdale, NJ: Lawrence Erlbaum Associates.

Goldin, G. A. (1987). Cognitive representational systems for mathematical problem solving. In C. Janvier (Ed.), *Problems of representation in the teaching and learning of mathematics* (pp. 125–145). Hillsdale, NJ: Lawrence Erlbaum Associates.

Greeno, J. G. (1983). Conceptual entities. In D. Gentner & A. L. Stevens (Eds.), *Mental models* (pp. 227–252). Hillsdale, NJ: Lawrence Erlbaum Associates.

Greeno, J. B., Riley, M. S., & Gelman, R. (1984). Conceptual competence and children's counting. *Cognitive Psychology, 16,* 94–143.

Hart, K. (1988). Ratio and proportion. In J. Hiebert & M. Behr (Eds.), *Research agenda for mathematics education: Number concepts and operations in the middle grades* (pp. 198–219). Reston, VA: National Council of Teachers of Mathematics.

Hatano, G., & Suga, Y. (1986, April). *A longitudinal study of subtraction bugs: An alternative view.* Paper presented at the annual meeting of the American Educational Research Association, San Francisco.

Hiebert, J. (1988). A theory of developing competence with written mathematical symbols. *Educational Studies in Mathematics, 19,* 333–355.

Hiebert, J. & Behr, M. (Eds.). (1988). *Research agenda for mathematics education: Number concepts and operations in the middle grades.* Reston, VA: National Council of Teachers of Mathematics.

Hiebert, J., & Lefevre, P. (1986). Conceptual and procedural knowledge in mathematics: An introductory analysis. In J. Hiebert (Ed.), *Conceptual and procedural knowledge: The case of mathematics* (pp. 1–27). Hillsdale, NJ: Lawrence Erlbaum Associates.

Hiebert, J., & Wearne, D. (1988). Instruction and cognitive change in mathematics. *Educational Psychologist, 23,* 105–117.

Hofstadter, D. R. (1979). *Gödel, Escher, Bach: An eternal golden braid.* New York: Vintage Books.

Kaput, J. J. (1987). Toward a theory of symbol use in mathematics. In C. Janvier (Ed.), *Problems of representation in the teaching and learning of mathematics* (pp. 159–195). Hillsdale, NJ: Lawrence Erlbaum Associates.

Kieren, T. E. (1988). Personal knowledge of rational number: Its intuitive and formal development. In J. Hiebert & M. Behr (Eds.), *Research agenda in mathematics education: Number concepts and operations in the middle grades* (pp. 162–181). Reston, VA: National Council of Teachers of Mathematics.

Kilpatrick, J. (1985). Reflection and recursion. *Educational Studies in Mathematics, 16,* 1–26.

Leinhardt, G., & Smith, D. A. (1985). Expertise in mathematics instruction: Subject matter knowledge. *Journal of Educational Psychology, 77,* 247–271.

Lesh, R., Post, T., & Behr, M. (1987). Representations and translations among representations in mathematics learning and problem solving. In C. Janvier (Ed.), *Problems of representation in the teaching and learning of mathematics* (pp. 33–40). Hillsdale, NJ: Lawrence Erlbaum Associates.

———. (1988). Proportional reasoning. In M. Behr & J. Hiebert (Ed.), *Research agenda for mathematics education: Number concepts and operations in the middle grades* (pp. 93–118). Reston, VA: National Council of Teachers of Mathematics.

Lindvall, C. M., & Ibarra, C. G. (1980). Incorrect procedures used by primary grade pupils in solving open addition and subtraction sentences. *Journal for Research in Mathematics Education, 11,* 50–62.

Mason, J. H. (1987). What do symbols represent? In C. Janvier (Ed.), *Problems of representation in the teaching and learning of mathematics* (pp. 73–81). Hillsdale, NJ: Lawrence Erlbaum Associates.

Nesher, P. (1988). Multiplicative school word problems: Theoretical approaches and empirical findings. In J. Hiebert & M. Behr (Eds.), *Research agenda for mathematics education: Number concepts and operations in the middle grades* (pp. 19–40). Reston, VA: National Council of Teachers of Mathematics.

Nesher, P., Greeno, J. G., & Riley, M. S. (1982). The development of semantic categories for addition and subtraction. *Educational Studies in Mathematics, 13,* 373–394.

Peterson, P. L., Fennema, E., Carpenter, T. P., & Loef, M. (1989). Teacher's pedagogical content beliefs in mathematics. *Cognition and Instruction, 6*(1), 1–40.

Post, T. R., Wachsmuth, I., Lesh, R., & Behr, M. J. (1985). Order and equivalence of rational numbers: A cognitive analysis. *Journal for Research in Mathematics Education, 16,* 18–36.

Putnam, R. T. (1987). Structuring and adjusting content for students: A study of live and simulated tutoring of addition. *American Educational Research Journal, 42,* 13–48.

Resnick, L. B. (1987). *Education and learning to think.* Washington, DC: National Academy Press.

Riley, M. S., Greeno, J. G., & Heller, J. I. (1983). Development of children's problem-solving ability in arithmetic. In H. P. Ginsburg (Ed.), *The development of mathematical thinking* (pp. 153–196). New York: Academic Press.

Romberg, T. A., & Carpenter, T. P. (1986). Research on teaching and learning mathematics: Two disciplines of scientific inquiry. In M. C. Wittrock (Ed.), *Correct Handbook of research on teaching* (3rd ed., pp. 850–873). New York: Macmillan.

Schoenfeld, A. H. (1988). When good teaching leads to bad results: The disasters of "well taught" mathematics courses. *Educational Psychologist, 23,* 145–166.

Shulman, L. S. (1986). Those who understand: Knowledge growth in teaching. *Educational Researcher, 15*(2), 4–14.

———. (1987). Knowledge and teaching: Foundations of the new reform. *Harvard Educational Review, 57,* 1–22.

Steffe, L. P. (1988). Children's construction of number sequences and multiplying schemes. In J. Hiebert & M. Behr (Eds.), *Research agenda in mathematics education: Number concepts and operations in the middle grades* (pp. 119–140). Reston, VA: National Council of Teachers of Mathematics.

Steffe, L. P., Thompson, P. W., & Richards, J. (1982). Children's counting in arithmetical problem solving. In T. P. Carpenter, J. M. Moser, & T. A. Romberg (Eds.), *Addition and subtraction: A cognitive perspective* (pp. 83–97). Hillsdale, NJ: Lawrence Erlbaum Associates.

Thompson, A. G. (1984). The relationship of teachers' conceptions of mathematics and mathematics teaching to instructional practice. *Educational Studies in Mathematics, 15,* 105–127.

Vergnaud, G. (1988). Multiplicative structures. In J. Hiebert & M. Behr (Eds.), *Research agenda for mathematics education: Number concepts and operations in the middle grades* (pp. 141–161). Reston, VA: National Council of Teachers of Mathematics.

Wearne, D. (1988, April). *Constructing meaning for decimal fraction symbols*. Paper presented at the annual meeting of the American Educational Research Association, New Orleans.

Wearne, D., & Hiebert, J. (1988). A cognitive approach to meaningful mathematics instruction: Testing a local theory using decimal numbers. *Journal for Research in Mathematics Education, 19,* 371–384.

7

Intermediate Teachers' Knowledge of Rational Number Concepts*

Thomas R. Post, Guershon Harel, Merlyn J. Behr, and Richard Lesh

The Rational Number Project (RNP) has been funded by the National Science Foundation (NSF) since 1979. The project originally involved three universities (Northern Illinois, Minnesota, and Northwestern) and utilized well-defined theory-based instructional and evaluation components as well as an overall plan for validating project-generated hypotheses. The project's earlier intent was to describe children's rational number development from its beginnings to its formal operational level in well-defined instructional settings. The major goal was the identification of psychological and mathematical variables which impede and/or promote the learning of rational number concepts. More recently (1984 – 88) the RNP has been focusing on the role of rational number concepts in the development of proportional reasoning skills. The current activity extends these beginnings to include work with in-service teachers in the

*This paper is based in part on research supported by the National Science Foundation under grants DPE-8470077 and TEI-8652341 (The Rational Number Project). Any opinions, findings, and conclusions expressed are those of the authors and do not necessarily reflect the views of the National Science Foundation. We wish to thank Sarah Currier and Nancy Williams for their invaluable assistance with the development, administration, and scoring of the teacher profile.

development of a model middle school mathematics teacher education program. A major objective is to develop and promote instructional leadership at the local level by retraining teams of teachers as master instructors and as providers of staff development for their peers. Theory-based materials and methods consistent with our previous work with children will be employed. Our formally stated objectives are:

a) To develop and conduct a model in-service teacher education program designed to enhance teacher understandings in important mathematical and pedagogical domains. The theoretical underpinnings of this work will be consistent with that of our previous work with children.

b) To conduct an assessment of the conceptions and misconceptions which elementary teachers have about mathematical topics germane to middle school mathematics programs. Assessment results will be compiled into mathematical knowledge profiles of teachers, similar to those we have generated for students. These profiles will then be used to guide development of other project components.

c) School-based teams of teachers will be retrained to become master teachers themselves and to function as members of a school-based leadership team with increasing responsibilities for staff development.

TEACHER EDUCATION AS AN EXTENSION
OF OUR EARLIER WORK

The assessment developed in this project for use with teachers is an attempt to apply the theoretical principles from our previous work with children. For example, the perceptual variability principle suggests that experiences provided should differ in outward appearance while retaining the same basic conceptual structure. Children often become sidetracked with irrelevant characteristics of a situation, especially when the grasp of the emerging concept is incomplete. Early conceptualizations are often distorted. This is as true for teachers as it is for children.

Teachers need to be exposed to aspects of the teaching act in a wide variety of conditions or contexts. For this reason, this project will focus on a broad spectrum of teacher roles (for example, as an instructor of large and small groups, as a tutor, as a student, as an interviewer, as a diagnostician, as a confidant, etc.) and relate these roles to the specific teaching-related tasks which teachers are expected to perform (Leinhardt & Greeno, 1986). Just as mathematical abstractions are themselves not contained in the materials which children use, it likewise seems true that abstractions and generalizations relating to the profession of teaching are not necessarily embedded in any single role which the teacher might assume. Such abstractions and generalizations can be gleaned only from overt consideration of a variety of situational, contextual, and model activities, roles, and tasks. Thus, in the same way that children are encouraged to discuss similarities and differences between various isomorphs of mathematical concepts, teachers will be encouraged to discuss similarities and differences between pedagogically related actions in various mathematical contexts. A wide variety of avenues will be exploited to provide the foundation for these discussions. Clinically based experiences, videotapes, demonstration lessons, and other types of sharing of experiences will be utilized during the 1988 – 89 school year. We hypothesize that it is the opportunity to examine a variety of situations from a number of perspectives and to gain the perspectives of other individuals that enables the development of pedagogically related higher order understandings and processes.

In the Applied Mathematical Problem Solving (AMPS) project, cooperative groups of intermediate-level children were asked to focus on a variety of mathematical models, concepts, and problem situations and then to discuss and come to agreement as to the intended meaning(s). See Figure 7-1a . Individual students were also asked to focus on several models or embodiments of a single mathematical idea and to indicate similarities and differences in the different interpretations (see figures 7-1 and 7-2). Later the

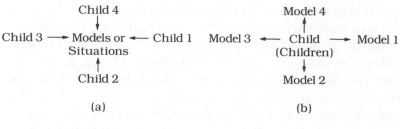

(a)   (b)

COOPERATIVE GROUPS   MULTIPLE EMBODIMENT

Figure 7-1. Other Interpretations of Multiple Perspectives

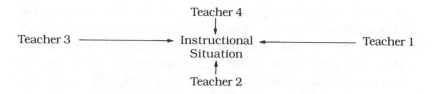

Figure 7-2. Additional Example of Multiple Perspectives

group task was to reconcile these interpretations in such a way as to arrive at the most probable (widely agreed upon) meaning. We believe that teachers can also profit from discussing single pedagogical incidents and attempting to reconcile the most probable meanings.

These two types of interactions can be viewed diagrammatically in figure 7-1. These models will be used directly with teachers and can also be extended to include instructional settings (figure 7-2). Notice that each of the situations presented in these figures is, in fact, a variation of the multiple embodiment principle applied to various patterns of human interaction.

In our earlier work with children, we continually attempted to stress higher order thinking and processes. Whether these related to rational number concepts or to issues regarding proportionality or mathematical problem solving, it was important to us to encourage children to go beyond the single incident and to reflect on general meanings. This invariably involved a process which has become known as "metacognition." We were encouraging children to think about their own thinking. In a similar fashion, it seems reasonable to encourage teachers to think seriously about the teaching acts of both themselves and others. The AMPS project determined that successful problem solvers tend to think at more than one level. These children were not only thinking about the problem at hand, they were also aware of their own thinking processes. The best problem solvers also attempted to "generalize" problem approaches, heuristics, and problem types in a manner similar to that described by Krutetskii (1976). The ability to be simultaneously the "doer" and the "observer" is critical to the solution of many multistage problems. Likewise, it seems important that teachers be able to identify behaviors at a number of levels as they occur in their own thinking.

Teachers not only teach content but also implicitly transmit attitudes and understandings about mathematics. Whether it is desirable or not, students think of teachers as models of "correct problem-solving behaviors." As teachers act out or demonstrate solutions to problems, it is especially important for them to be able to reflect on their own problem-solving behaviors and to help students identify their own metacognitive processes. The ability to accurately and insightfully observe one's own problem-solving behavior may be closely related to the ability to accurately observe, describe, and critique the problem-solving behavior of others.

A third major aspect of the model suggested here includes the provision of experiences focused on an integration of content, pedagogy, and psychology. That is, the mathematical content discussed will be presented in a manner which reflects sound psychological principles using research-validated teaching techniques (Good & Grouws, 1977, 1979).

In the same way that the ten basic skills suggested by the National Council of Supervisors of Mathematics in 1978 (problem solving, estimation, approximation, graphical analysis, etc.) cannot be taught effectively in isolation from one another, the teaching act cannot be separated from the mathematical content which it is intended to convey nor from the psychological overtones which human beings tend to impose on cognitive schema. The following example suggesting a coordination of the content and psychological dimensions arises from our previous work with children. Our observations suggest that children whose rational number concepts are insecure tend to have a continuing interference from their whole number schemas. This interference needs careful consideration by teachers. Clearly it would be inadequate simply to inform children when the schemata they have developed for dealing with whole numbers are appropriate and when they are not; children need to learn how to make such determinations on their own.

There are also times when various mathematical domains can be related to one another. For example, the solution of a missing value problem ($a/b : c/x$), the generation of equivalent fractions, and the generation of a second ratio reflecting an equal probability have much in common. Likewise the unit rate in a proportional situation can be related to the slope (m) of a linear function with an equation of the form $y = mx$. Many other examples exist.

An example implying a relationship between content and pedagogy arises from the work of Robert Davis (personal communication, August, 1985). Davis suggests that new concepts should be introduced in a manner which establishes an "assimilation paradigm" or a conceptual framework to which future variations can be compared and contrasted. Applied to the part-whole interpretation of rational numbers, this suggests that initial concepts be solidified within a single perspective (for example, circular pieces) before others are introduced (for example, Cuisenaire rods, number lines, chips, etc.). Kieren (1976) has suggested that early (part-whole) embodiments or interpretations also serve the function of helping to establish an appropriate semantic and definitional structure. These are of course necessary for extension to related domains. Thus, a technique for teaching new content emerges, one which integrates mathematical structures with sound pedagogical teaching. Such techniques are based on validated psychological principles of conceptual development. Many similar examples can be extracted from our work and the work of others.

The parallels existing between previously understood work with children and processes important to effective teaching hold great promise for teacher education. Our attempt to translate these understandings from one domain to the other will provide a context within which the development of project components can be both understood and fostered.

THE MATHEMATICAL KNOWLEDGE
PROFILES OF TEACHERS

A major objective of this project is the generation of profiles of mathematical understandings for teachers, similar to those we have generated for students. We then intend to create teacher training materials based in part on these profiles and in part on the same principles of learning and instruction that we have validated for youngsters.

We know from pilot investigations (for example, Lesh & Schultz, 1983; Post et al., 1985) that many of the same misunderstandings and "naive conceptualizations" that we have identified in youngsters also are prevalent among teachers. Yet, we really do not know very much about what mathematics intermediate level (grades 4 – 6) teachers actually do know and understand. The knowledge profile is a theory-based assessment focused on generating profiles of teachers' content understandings. Part 1 consists of short answer items, Part 2 requests pedagogical explanations of solutions generated, and Part 3 consists of a two-hour interview, all relating to rational number concepts: part-whole, decimals, ratios and percents, proportionality, and multiplication and division.

Part 1 had two longer versions (A & B) which consisted of seventy-eight short answer items. The two shorter versions (AA & BB) each contained fifty-eight items. Seventy-five minutes was allotted for the teachers to complete Part 1. It was possible to gather a wider variety of information by developing multiple versions which had some items in common. Table 2 below provides the means for the Minnesota site for Part 1 of the instrument. All versions contained items dealing with very fundamental notions about fractions and decimals.

Part 1 also contained 17 items which were one-step multiplication and division problems. These problems addressed hypotheses relating to partitive and quotative division and to achievement levels as a function of the relative sizes of divisor, dividend, and quotient. One test version had items which dealt with nonintegral numbers in fraction form, the other version contained parallel items but contained decimals rather than fractions. There were seventeen items of each type. Fourteen were partitive or quotative division, and three involved multiplication. Table 1 indicates the number of items dealing with each subtopic

Table 7-1

Teacher Profile Part 1 Number of Items Per Subtopic

Topic	Number of Items	Topic	Number of Items
Part Whole	2	Concept of Unit	4
Ordering:		Estimation	5
a) decimals	2	Ratio	5
b) fractions	4	Numerical Comparison	3
c) miscellaneous	3	1979 NAEP Word Problems	3
Equivalence	4	Division: Partitive &	
"Qualitative Thinking"	3	Quotative	14*
Percent	3	Multiplication:	
Operations:		One-step problems	3*
a) decimals	5	Missing Value	4
b) fractions	13		
c) conversions	3		

*Fraction or decimal

of Part 1. A given test version does not contain all item categories.

Part 2 of the assessment contained three versions (C, D, and E). Each contained six problems, which requested that the teacher provide as much information as possible relative to their thought processes, solution procedures, etc. Many Part 2 items also asked for some indication of how this information would be taught to children. Version C contained types of problems: (*a*) partitive division, (*b*) missing value, (*c*) one-step multiplication with fraction as multiplier and multiplicand, (*d*) one-step division containing decimals, (*e*) a new kind of project-developed problem, currently referred to as an effect problem, and (*f*) finding the unit rate given two decimals. Results of type f problems will be discussed in this paper. Version D also contained six problems: (*a*) a numerical comparison problem with equivalent fractions, (*b*) a quotative division problem with fractional numbers as entries, (*c*) a concept of unit problem with chips, (*d*) a more difficult effect problem, (*e*) a quotative division word problem with fractions less than one, and (*f*) a word problem involving ratios. The Illinois site utilized a third version dealing with other aspects of order, equivalence, and ratio.

Part 3 of our Teacher Profile consists of a structured interview. This interview was related to Parts 1 and 2. We attempted to interview teachers in each third of the distribution of scores on Part 1. In Illinois and in Minnesota fifteen interviews, each lasting from two to two and a half hours, were conducted. The interviews, although structured in nature, provided flexibility for the individual interviewer to pursue questioning lines of interest. In Minnesota four persons were interviewed both before and after participation in the 1988 four-week Summer Leadership Institute.

Subjects. At the Minnesota site, seventeen elementary schools were involved in Parts 1 and 2 of the assessment. This represented two thirds of the twenty-seven schools with an intermediate level (4 – 6) program from a single large urban district. Only teachers who had current responsibility for mathematics instruction in grades 4, 5, or

6 were included. All teachers at this level in a given school were required to participate in both Parts 1 and 2 of the profile. There were, of course, several instances of teacher absence, but the numbers here were very small and felt to be of no particular significance. In all, 167 teachers participated in the Minnesota testing, and 51 teachers were involved at the Illinois site. A similar process was used in Illinois, although with a larger number of smaller rural school districts.

Results. Table 7-2 provides the mean, median, and range for Minnesota teachers for the two versions of the seventy-eight-item test, and the two versions of the fifty-eight-item test. Minnesota teachers scored between 60 and 69 percent correct, depending on the test version. Versions B and BB contained a heavier emphasis on missing value, numerical comparison, and ratio-related problems, and on these versions, teachers' scores were slightly lower.

Table 7-3 contains the mean percentage correct by item category. To provide some indication of the kind of questions asked, we have chosen to include the item with the highest percentage correct and the item with the lowest percentage correct within each category. This is done for each site.

These results are quite disconcerting! The items were developed to reflect what we believe to be the conceptual underpinnings of rational number topics for grades, 4, 5, and 6. We included the subsections on operations with fractions and decimals almost as an afterthought and in an attempt to document that the teachers are thoroughly conversant with precisely those types of items that are in the 4 through 6 curriculum. This was not the case. Ten to 25 percent of the teachers missed items which we feel were at the most rudimentary level. In some cases, almost half the teachers missed very fundamental items (that is, $1/3 \div 3$ [posed vertically] was answered correctly by only 54 percent of the teachers).

The remaining categories of items were adapted from some of our earlier work with children and our attempts to identify several of the more important topical areas related

Table 7-2

Rational Number Project: Teacher Profile Part 1 Results:
Minneapolis Site: April 1988

Test Version	N	Total Possible	Range	Median	Mean	Mean Percent Correct
A	30	78	12–76	53	50	64
B	30	78	19–72	46	47	60
AA	52	58	5–58	44	40	69
BB	55	58	14–56	38	38	66

Table 7-3

Percent Correct By Item Category and Site From Teacher Profile
Part 1

Item Category	Number of Items	Item with Highest % Correct	Item with Lowest % Correct	Mean Percent Correct for All Items in Category
Part Whole:				
U. of M.:	2	Given 4 of 12 circles shaded: Shade equivalent fraction on blank circle provided. (81.3)*	Show circle with $7/8$ shaded: Ask: what part shaded? (65.3) (20.4% said $1/8$)	73.3
N.I.U.:	2	same problem (73.1)	same problem (54.9)	64
Ordering Fractions:				
U. of M.:	4	Write fraction between $7/8$ and 1 (76.0)	Order smallest to largest: $5/8$, $3/10$, $3/5$, $1/4$, $2/3$, $1/2$ (1979 NAEP item) (50.3)	65.3
N.I.U.:	4	same problem (86.3)	same problem (60.8)	69.9

Item Category	Number of Items	Item with Highest % Correct	Item with Lowest % Correct	Mean Percentage Correct for All Items in Category
Ordering Decimals:				
U. of M.:	2	Order from smallest to largest: .3, .3157, .32, 1316 (58.7)	Write decimal between 3.1 and 3.11 (49.7)	54.2
N.I.U.	2	same problem (80.4)	same problem (64.7)	72.6
Misc. Ordering:				
U. of M.:	3	$\frac{7}{12} = \frac{1}{2} + \underline{\hspace{1cm}}$ (88.5)	What number is one third of way between $\frac{1}{2}$ and $\frac{7}{8}$? (53.6)	68.9
N.I.U.:	3	same problem (80)	Order 5 fractions, or their representation. (47.1)	65.4
Fraction equivalence:				
U. of M.:	4	$\frac{8}{14} = \underline{\hspace{1cm}} / 21$ (61.1)	$\frac{8}{15} = \underline{\hspace{1cm}} / 5$ (35.3)	49.7
N.I.U.:	4	$\frac{4}{6} = \frac{6}{\underline{\hspace{1cm}}}$ (66.7)	same problem (31.4)	51
Qualitative Thinking:				
U. of M.:	3	What will happen to the value of the fraction a/b if "a" is increased four times and "b" is halved? (42.4)	What happens to $\frac{9}{8}$ if numerator tripled and denominator divided by 4? 6 choices (29.4)	37.7
N.I.U.:	3	same problem (64)	same problem (28)	

Item Category	Number of Items	Item with Highest % Correct	Item with Lowest % Correct	Mean Percent Correct for All Items in Category
Concept of Unit:				
U. of M.:	4	Full lot with 18 cars red, which is ⅓ of lot. How many cars in all? (86.7)	If 000 000 = ½ of unit, how many in unit? (54.5)	69.6
N.I.U.:	3	Given 9 circles, which represent ¾ of unit, determine # circles in ⅔ of same unit. (78.4)	9 circles are ⁸/₇ of a unit. How many in unit? (64)	69.7
Estimation: (Form A)				
U. of M.:	5	Estimate product 47 × 2.17. Choose 1, 9, 100, .08, .01 (79.3)	Place decimal point in correct position. 4.5 × 51.26. 0 2 3 0 6 7 0 0 (64.6)	70.9
N.I.U.:	4	same problem (92.3)	same problem (61.5)	76.9
Ratio:				
U. of M.:	5	Given 15 squares and fact ratio of blue to red is 2:3. How many blue? (49.1)	Given 243 parts made in 9 hours. One makes 13 in an hour, how many 2nd person makes in an hour. (47.8)	47.7

Item Category	Number of Items	Item with Highest % Correct	Item with Lowest % Correct	Mean Percent Correct for All Items in Category
N.I.U.:	4	Ratio men to women is 3:5. How many women if 120 men? (69.2)	Given 15 blue and red squares and fact ratio of blue to red is 2:3, how many blue? (46.2)	55.9
Percent				
U. of M.:	3	What is 40% of 80? (75.6)	75 is what percent of 60? (57.3)	64.2
N.I.U.:	3	same problem (96)	same problem (54)	76
Operations with Fractions:				
U. of M.:	13	$16\frac{3}{5}$ (89.2)	$\frac{1}{3} + 3$ (53.6)	73.7
N.I.U.:	13	same problem (96.1)	$3 + \frac{4}{3}$ (40)	71.0
Operations with Decimal:				
U. of M.:	5	Subtract $3.1 - .4$ (97.3)	$1000 + 1000 + .01$ (86.6)	91.8
N.I.U.:	3	same problem (96.2)	$86 - .3$ (80.0)	90.1
Conversions:				
U. of M.:	3	Write $14\frac{1}{4}$ as mixed numeral (98.3)	Express $\frac{7}{25}$ in decimal form (73.7)	84.5
N.I.U.:	1	—	same problem (63)	62.7
Numerical Comparison:				
U. of M.:	3	Given 2 rates. Compare: Equivalent (87.1)	Given 2 rates, compare: part of rate is fraction. Noninteger multiple (70.4)	77.6

Item Category	Number of Items	Item with Highest % Correct	Item with Lowest % Correct	Mean Percent Correct for All Items in Category
N.I.U.:	2	same problem (92)	similar problem (88)	90.0

1979 NAEP Word Problems:

Item Category	Number of Items	Item with Highest % Correct	Item with Lowest % Correct	Mean Percent Correct for All Items in Category
U. of M.:	3	17 year old mean percent correct (3 problems) (59.8)	13 year old mean percent correct (2 problems) (23.2)	42.6
N.I.U.:	2	— (76.9)	— (38.5)	57.7 (Teacher Means)

*Percent correct by site in parentheses.

to, and necessary for, the development of proportional reasoning abilities. Overall mean scores of less than 70 percent certainly do not imply overall teacher "mastery" of these topical domains. Of course, some teachers did relatively well. Many did not.

Perhaps more troubling than overall means are the distribution patterns identified within the various item clusters. Regardless of which item category is selected, a significant percentage of teachers were missing one-half to two-thirds of the items. This percentage varied by category, but in general 20 to 30 percent of the teachers scored less than 50 percent on the overall instrument.

It was not our intention to assess only what teachers do and do not know, but rather to try to understand the way in which teachers understand these important ideas.

For example, each of the three versions of Part 2 of the teacher profile consisted of six questions in a word problem format. Teachers were asked to solve the problem, and then to indicate how they would explain their solution to a child who did not yet have the concepts involved. Our intent was twofold: first, to determine whether teachers could themselves solve the problems, and second, to determine the conceptual and pedagogical adequacy of the explanations which they provided. Responses were categorized across six major variables:

1. Answer—correct or incorrect, common errors
2. Solution strategy—types
3. Explanation—adequacy of logical structure and flow of explanation
4. Procedural vs. Conceptual
5. Reference to diagram/model—supportive, nonsupportive
6. Checking—explain procedures for

Each of these categories invariably contained multiple (usually five to eight) subclassifications depending on the particular problem. These subclassifications can be observed in the next set of tables. Shulman's category of content knowledge as well as his category of pedagogical content knowledge were of concern to us (Shulman, 1986).

The problems were adaptations from our previous work with children, and were primarily concerned with areas of rational number and proportionality. For the most part they were not precisely the type of problem which appears in the intermediate grade curriculum, and would more probably be found at the junior high level. We feel strongly, however, that a firm grasp of the underlying concepts is an important and necessary framework for the elementary teacher to possess, especially those who are teaching related concepts to children in the intermediate grades.

Figure 7-3 indicates results of this analysis applied to a problem concerned with finding a unit rate. Note the subclassifications referred to earlier. This problem was administered to approximately half of the teachers at the Minnesota site. (N = 77)

As noted above, less than half (44.7 percent) of the teachers were able to solve this problem correctly. Strategies used range from crisp accurate processes to laments such as "this is a very tricky problem," this latter response followed by a blank sheet. In addition, only a small percentage (10.5) of those able to solve the problem correctly pro-

Figure 7.0

Problem: Marissa bought 0.46 of a pound of wheat flour for which she paid $0.83. How many pounds of flour could she buy for one dollar?

# 1 Answer Subclassifications	Percent
0 = Wrong	15.8
1 = Correct (.55 or rounded approximation)	44.7
2 = 2¼	2.6
3 = 1.80, 1.82, 1.85 (result of .83 − .46)	3.6
4 = .65	2.6
8 = Computational Error	2.6
9 = Blank or "Don't Know"	27.6

# 2 Solution Strategy	Percent
0 = Ratio scalar approach $$\frac{.46 \times 012 = .55}{.83 \times 012 = 1.00}$$	—
1 = Ratio, cross-multiply $$\frac{.46}{.83} = \frac{x}{1.00} \text{ or } \frac{.46}{x} = \frac{.83}{1.00}$$	27.6
2 = Ratio, *set-up but unable to solve*	5.3
3 = Divide .83 ÷ .46 *no set up proportion*	3.9
4 = Divide .46 ÷ .83 *no set up proportion*	6.6
5 = Use simpler numbers, solve, then do same with problem	7.9
6 = *Incorrect* arithmetic manipulations of numbers $1 - .83 = \_\_\_$, $1 - .46 = \_\_\_$, $.46 \times 2 = \_\_\_$, etc.	—
7 = Estimate first to decide	3.9
8 = Other, including bluffs	15.8
9 = Blank—completely blank pages or problems with answer, *nothing* further	28.9

#3 Explanation	Percent
1 = Adequate	10.5
2 = Inadequate = for *wrong* answers only	10.5
3 = Partial/Sketchy/On the track/any correct answer with *very little* explanation	28.9

4 = Garbled/confusing/hard to follow	9.2
8 = Bluff	6.6
9 = Blank—completely blank pages or problems with answer and *nothing* further	34.2

#4 Procedural vs. Conceptual	Percent
0 = Procedural only	30.3
1 = Conceptual invoked	1.3
3 = Partial ... evidence of both	27.6
8 = Bluff	7.9
9 = Blank—completely blank pages or problems with answer, *nothing* further	32.9

#5 Diagram/Model	Percent
0 = No reference	65.8
1 = Supportive—complete (correct)	
2 = Supportive—incomplete (correct)	1.3
3 = Non-supportive reference (*incorrect*)	
9 = Blank—for completely blank pages or problems with answer, *nothing* further	32.9

#6 Checking	Percent
1 = Plug answer in for unknown in ratio	26.3
2 = Round numbers to see if answer seems about right (½ # for $.83 so .55# for $1.00 makes sense)	5.3
3 = "Don't know"	—
8 = Other/bluff/wrong	14.5
9 = Blank	53.9

vided what was considered a coherent, rational, and pedagogically "acceptable" explanation. (Recall that teachers were asked to explain their solutions to a child.)

Similar results were obtained for the majority of the other Part 2 questions. There were three versions of Part 2, each containing six questions; two were administered in Minnesota, the other in Illinois. Thus there exists data on eighteen such problems.

Table 7-4 presents summative statistics relating to twelve of the eighteen Part 2 questions referred to above. Notice the large percentage of reliance on procedural expla-

Table 7-4

Part 2 Pedagogically Related Results

Version C

Problem	% Correct	Adequate Explanation	Procedural/ Conceptual Explanation	Blank Answers
1	78.9	53.9	6.6/50.0	5.3
2	69.7	27.6	43.4/5.3	7.9
3A	55.2	14.5	6.6/14.5	22.4
3B	28.3	13.2	15.1/13.2	24.5
4 (Marissa)	44.7	10.5	30.3/1.3	27.6
5	60.5	14.5	10.5/43.4	35.5
6	17.1	7.9	42.1/10.5	31.6
Averages:	50.6	20.3	22.1	

N = 76

Version D

Problem	% Correct	Adequate Explanation	Procedural/ Conceptual Explanation	Blank Answers
1	7.57	37.8	55.4/20.3	4.1
2	41.9	20.3	33.8/13.5	21.6
3A	73.0	31.1	51.4/9.5	12.2
3B	68.9	—	—	13.5
4	35.1	20.3	27.0/6.8	23.0
5	54.1	20.3	24.3/14.9	20.3
6	81.1	32.4	45.9/14.9	13.5
Averages:	61.4	27.0	15.5	

N = 74

nations and also the significant percentage of teachers who did not attempt to solve the problems. These were recorded in the blank answer column.

Our results indicate that a multilevel problem exists. The first and primary one is the fact that many teachers simply do not know enough mathematics. The second is that only a minority of those teachers who are able to solve these problems correctly are able to explain their solutions in a pedagogically acceptable manner; in the Marissa problem this was 10.5 percent. The average of pedagogically acceptable explanations for the 44.7% of the teachers who were able to compute the correct results was 20.3% for version C and 27% for version D. The Illinois results are not yet available.

Most assessments of student's mathematical performance (NAEP, SIMS, etc.) have indicated that our young people simply do not have the desired level of competence, especially as that competence relates to higher order mathematical understandings and processes. We must now begin to ask more deeply about the potential interactions between teachers' mathematical understandings and the achievement levels of their students.

As mathematics educators continue to attempt to improve presecondary mathematics programs, principally by expanding the scope of appropriate components (problem solving, estimation, geometry, computers, etc.), we must realize that we are asking a significant percentage of teachers to teach concepts to which they themselves were never exposed as students. Add to this the uneven quality of both the mathematics and methods preservice experiences provided (one of our teachers said her entire methods course was spent evaluating textbooks, another that her mathematics course consisted almost entirely of base-12 arithmetic), and these results become perhaps more understandable, although certainly not more acceptable. Further, consider the wide variety of noncurricular related "add-ons" which have found their way into the elementary school curriculum, and a problem of immense proportions becomes apparent. What also becomes apparent is the enormous complexity of the task of being an elementary school teacher.

It seems feasible for us as a professional research community to urge large scale consideration of alternative delivery systems as well as alternative school organizational patterns and to carefully identify the implications each would have on the structure and substance of elementary school mathematics program. We must be very careful to make these recommendations in the most constructive and positive way possible. We are convinced that teachers are also very interested in substantive progress.

While it may not be possible to produce a sufficiently

large number of "experts" for the intermediate level mathematics classroom, we fail to understand how teachers without a relatively firm foundation could possibly be in a position to present and explain properly, to ask the right question at the right time, and to recognize and encourage high levels of student mathematical thinking when it occurs. Mathematics courses in teacher education programs, especially preservice mathematics courses, to date, have generally been concerned with rather superficial treatment of lofty content domains rather than a relatively deep treatment of elementary topical areas. The latter type of involvement seems appealing to us. Much work would need to be done to "flesh out" the precise nature of such a deep treatment. Two such elementary topical domains which come immediately to mind are additive and multiplicative structures (Vergnaud, 1983). A sizable amount of research has been conducted in each of these, but so far the emphasis has not been on the development of the appropriate teacher-based learning activities. Some of the subcategories on this instrument may be a reasonable starting point within the domain of multiplicative structures.

As this work progresses it will be necessary to rethink the entire elementary school mathematics curriculum. Adequate student understandings will need to be developed over a long period of time and in a manner quite different than is currently being done. As these broader and deeper teacher understandings are identified and developed, the direction of curricular revision will become more clear.

It may be that computer-assisted instruction will have a significant impact on helping both teachers and students to develop these broader and deeper understandings. Teachers and students learning side by side seems a reasonable scenario. Although few of these software packages currently exist, there are some notable examples. The IBM Mathematics Tool Kit, which is a full-scale algebraic manipulator and function plotter, is one. The Geometric Supposers are others. Examples are more difficult to identify at the elementary school level. These new utilities, when developed and implemented, will, over time, significantly influence the ways in which teachers interact with children about mathematics. We as a community need to talk seriously about the implications which these results have for teacher reeducation programs.

REFERENCES

Good, T. L., & Grouws, D. A. (1977). Teaching effects: A process-product study in fourth grade mathematics classrooms. *Journal of Teacher Education, 28*, (May–June, 1977), 49–54.

―――. (1979). The Missouri mathematics effectiveness project: An experimental study in fourth grade classrooms. *Journal of Educational Psychology, 71* (July, 1979), 355–362.

Kieren, T. (1976). On the mathematical, cognitive and instructional foundations of rational numbers. In *Number and measurement: Papers from a research workshop* (pp. 101–144). Columbus, OH: ERIC/SMEAC.

Krutetskii, V. (1976). *The psychology of mathematical abilities in school children.* Chicago: University of Chicago Press.

Leinhart, G., & Greeno, J. G. (1986). The cognitive skill of teaching. *Journal of Educational Psychology, 78*, 75–79.

Lesh, R. A., & Schultz, K. (1983, September). Teacher characterizations of students' problem solving episodes. In J. C. Bergeron, & N. Herscovics (Eds.), *Proceedings of the Fifth Annual Meeting of the North American Chapter of the International Group for the Psychology of Mathematics Learning* (pp. 00–00). Montreal, Canada.

National Council of Supervisors of Mathematics (February, 1978). Position Paper on Basic Skills. *Mathematics Teacher, 71*, 147–52.

Post, T. R., Behr, M. J., Lesh, R., & Wachsmuth, I. (1985). Selected results from the rational number project. In L. Streefland (Ed.), *Proceedings of the Ninth International Conference for the Psychology of Mathematics Education Volume 1: Individual Contributions* (pp. 342–351). Noordwijkerhout, The Netherlands: International Group for the Psychology of Mathematics Education.

Shulman, L. S. (1986). Those who understand: Knowledge growth in teaching. *Educational Research, 15*(2), 4–14.

Vergnaud, G. (1983). Multiplicative structures. In R. Lesh & M. Landau (Eds.), *Acquisition of mathematics concepts and processes* (pp. 127–174). Orlando, FL: Academic Press.

8

Improving Research in Mathematics Classroom Instruction*

Douglas A. Grouws

Researchers in mathematics education are once again reflecting on the paradigms, methods, and theoretical frameworks they employ (Grouws, Cooney, & Jones, 1988). Recent discussions have emphasized the need to consider research on mathematics learning and research on mathematics teaching concomitantly in designing studies and building models of classroom mathematics instruction (Carpenter & Fennema, 1988). This approach seems appropriate because each area is substantively related to classroom events. How researchers can take both areas into account in meaningful ways is not immediately apparent. Past research indicates that theories of teaching do not follow directly from theories of learning. Similarly, how to use knowledge about how learners acquire mathematical competence in specific content domains to plan instruction is not obvious. Hence, researchers are confronted with a significant problem to which there is no immediate solution. (The problem needs further study.)

In this chapter, I suggest possible methods of productively drawing on research in teaching and learning with the hope that future research will be more insightful and

---

*This paper is based in part on research supported by the National Science Foundation under grant No. MDR-847-0265. All opinions expressed herein are solely those of the author.

helpful. The paper discusses the following areas: teachers as thoughtful decision makers, expanding teachers' knowledge, the role of knowledge about effective teaching practice, how teachers affect learning, key components in teaching/learning paradigms, models of teacher decision making, quality of instruction, and compromise in classroom instruction.

Teachers as Thoughtful Decision Makers

There is consensus that good teachers should be reflective, thoughtful decision makers (Carpenter & Fennema, 1988; Clark & Peterson, 1986). Further, teachers make decisions in complex environments that involve considerable uncertainty (Shavelson & Stern, 1981; Shulman & Elstein, 1975). The fact that teachers make carefully considered decisions has implications for planning and conducting research, especially research that involves training sessions for teachers where the effects of these workshops are later assessed in the classroom.

Several recent studies (Carpenter, Fennema, Peterson, Chiang, & Loef, 1988; Cobb, Wood, & Yackel, in press) have provided teachers with information from research on student learning and have studied the effects of this acquired teacher knowledge in first- and second-grade classrooms. The nature of the information conveyed to teachers varies from study to study. On the one hand, the Carpenter, Fennema, Peterson, Chiang, & Loef (1988) study made detailed and specific information available to teachers in the initial phase of the investigation. This information provided in-depth knowledge about student learning gathered from research in a specific mathematical content domain (basic addition and subtraction). On the other hand, the Cobb, Wood, & Yackel (in press) study made available to teachers information from a particular philosophical perspective about the nature of knowledge and how it is acquired. The underlying belief in both studies is that teachers, as thoughtful and reflective professionals, will use the knowledge or perspective gained from such training sessions in making classroom decisions. Thus, it is expected that substantive changes will be found in the nature of the mathematics instruction and student learning taking place in these classrooms. An important corollary of this position is that although not all teachers will make the same decisions, there will be some commonality, and, that analyses of teacher decisions will reflect the knowledge/perspective attended to in the training sessions.

One important issue raised by the Carpenter, Fennema, Peterson, Chiang, & Loef (1988) research is the extent to which teachers make classroom decisions on the basis of the information they gather about student learning and the particular mental states of the students in the class, and to what degree other factors affect their decisions. Other factors might include instructional expectations that teachers glean from the information researchers indirectly and unintentionally convey, as well as specific ideas, guidelines, techniques, and so on, that they might like to see implemented in subsequent mathematics lessons. Given the substantial length of some information sessions, it does not seem unrealistic that researchers would communicate some expectations about teacher classroom behavior. For example, the need to listen carefully to students and spend substantial time on problem-solving work might easily be indirectly communicated.

Communication of such expectations is not detrimental; in fact, the contrary may be true. What must be avoided is assuming that such information is *not* communicated to teachers as part of experimental treatments and that teachers do not put forth considerable effort to implement that advice. If the preceding scenario is true, then it may be appropriate to make such instructional guidelines explicit and discuss their appropriate use or misuse as part of the training. Considering that teachers are reasonable and thoughtful — and I fully subscribe to that position — it follows that a discussion of such guidelines would have numerous advantages. I suspect, however, that this tack could be misinterpreted and mistakenly labeled a prescription.

This would be unfortunate. Surely, thoughtful and reflective teachers can take clearly stated advice and suggestions and use them selectively and appropriately.

In summary, the concept of teachers as reflective practitioners is useful and should pervade the planning, conducting, and interpreting of research. To do otherwise, or to use the concept selectively only when it is convenient to an argument at hand causes problems, and the concept is too valuable to diminish in that way. Finally, descriptions of the nature of the information sessions conducted for teachers as part of research studies should err on the side of providing too much detail. Rich description is preferred to delineating the character of these meetings by using dichotomies such as training versus education, or teaching versus programming teachers. When such labels are used, they have too many values inherently associated with them to be helpful in interpreting or replicating the associated research. Careful description of the training (information) sessions is needed.

Expanding Teachers' Knowledge

Historically, general teacher knowledge has been identified by both researchers and practitioners as an important component of successful teaching, but it has been difficult to quantitatively document its value. In the last decade, due to the work of Shulman and others, discussions of teacher knowledge have become more refined and productive as various types of knowledge have been identified. For example, Shulman (1986) distinguishes between subject-matter content knowledge, pedagogical knowledge, and curriculum knowledge. Subject-matter content knowledge is defined to be that comprehension of subject matter that would be appropriate to a subject-matter specialist (for example, a person who majored in mathematics). Pedagogical knowledge goes beyond subject-matter knowledge to the dimension of subject-matter knowledge for teaching. It includes awareness of various means of representing ideas, important examples and counterexamples, illuminating analogies, common student errors and misconceptions, and so on. Curriculum knowledge involves an awareness of alternative textbooks and their approaches, available software, films and videotapes, and an understanding of the levels of complexity and the potential usefulness of each of these in a variety of situations. Providing teachers with detailed, accurate knowledge of the preceding types should assist them in making good instructional decisions and be valuable to them in planning and conducting instruction. Indeed, this is a basic premise of the Cognitively Guided Instruction (CGI) model (Carpenter & Fennema, 1988). It is not surprising, therefore, that teacher knowledge is a prominent part of their study in first-grade classrooms dealing with addition and subtraction concepts (Carpenter, Fennema, Peterson, Chiang, & Loef, 1988). Two issues need to be considered as additional research of this type is conducted: what knowledge do teachers need, and how should it be provided.

The Role of Knowledge About Effective Teaching Practice

There is currently little disagreement about the value of investigating teacher knowledge of student learning in specific content domains. What receives considerably less attention is the value of providing information from research about teaching, especially teaching that is linked to valued student outcomes.

Teachers are decision makers who make a large number of important decisions daily. They need to make these decisions with full knowledge of the research on teaching, as well as the research on student learning. Current research focuses merely on the relationship between teachers' decisions and their assessment of students' thinking. Sufficient attention is not given to other information on which teachers should, and do, rely. It seems logical that many decisions should be based, in part, on teachers' knowledge and beliefs that are not content-specific. For example, teachers should use information concerning classroom management, classroom organization, time allocation, and past instruction, both in planning instruction and in making in-class instructional decisions.

To illustrate how such factors may influence decision making, consider the issue of allocation of mathematics class time. If teachers place students in small groups for mathematics instruction so that they can benefit from interaction with peers, explore situations in a nonthreatening atmosphere, and improve their ability to communicate mathematically, then teachers should consider knowledge that has accumulated from previous classroom research on grouping in mathematics before implementing this decision. For example, teachers should provide for systematic review and maintenance of important skills and ideas that have been developed. Consideration of how much time is spent on development would be important, as would the amount of time spent on practice. Similarly, teachers should consider whether groups should operate in a competitive or cooperative atmosphere, and the implications of spending large portions of class time giving directions to get groups started on tasks or going over previous practice work. These are just some of the important factors identified by previous research on mathematics teaching that should be given careful thought as teachers make decisions.

Future discussions on the value of providing information to teachers from research on teaching should center on the potential value of such knowledge for teachers. Subsequent discussion should focus on what knowledge this might include and also identify areas where additional research is needed. It seems counterproductive at this point to engage in a debate about whether there is sufficient knowledge in this area or not. If there is not, and such knowledge is needed, then this is an important agenda for research.

In summary, if researchers are indeed serious about using results from both teaching and learning research to conduct better studies of classroom learning and improve student achievement, then we need to examine how information gathered from research on teaching can be used by thoughtful teachers to create classroom conditions that foster meaningful student learning. Further, we need to incorporate this information into treatment programs equally with information from research on student learning.

How Teachers Affect Learning

Current discussion attributes considerable importance to the role of the teacher in classroom mathematics learning, and it is imperative that researchers continue to emphasize this role. It was not that many years ago that attempts to develop teacher-proof curricula appeared, first in the form of programmed learning materials, then in the textbooks of the modern mathematics era, and more recently by the use of technology. If researchers do not emphasize the teacher's role, teacher effects will again be deemphasized, giving way to some other current but ephemeral fad.

Since what teachers do (and don't do) in the classroom affects student learning, developing a deep understanding of this influence should be a high priority for researchers. A major focus of the Wisconsin research program involves teachers' use of specific pedagogical content knowledge to assess student understanding, and the further use of the data from these assessments to make instructional decisions. This is an important direction for research, but additional focuses are needed to achieve the goal of understanding precisely how teachers promote classroom learning.

Teaching is a complex phenomenon and a variety of teacher decisions influence student learning. The knowledge and beliefs that teachers draw on in making these decisions do not necessarily rely exclusively on knowledge of individual student's content-specific knowledge. Classroom management decisions, for example, are probably based on a general assessment of classroom conditions and a teacher's beliefs and knowledge about productive classroom environments. Decisions about instructional organization are another example. Teachers often make decisions about how to group children on the basis of general student achievement (Good, Grouws, & Mason, 1990). What questions to ask and what student to call on may also be dictated by a host of factors that are not dependent on content-specific pedagogical knowledge of individual students. The general nature of teachers' beliefs about learners, the nature of instruction, and teachers' conceptions of mathematics, to name a few areas, affect instructional decision making. They need to be an integral part of future research on teacher decision making in mathematics classrooms.

Key Components in Teaching/Learning Paradigms

As major new research programs emerge, an abundance of questions always arise and need exploration. Three questions that should receive some priority readily come to mind. First, how does the new knowledge teachers acquire affect their beliefs and conceptualizations? Do teachers initially come to realize that there are additional perspectives other than their own, or do they become more receptive to new perspectives? Do teachers adopt new perspectives by abandoning one previously held, or do they initially entertain them simultaneously, using one or another depending on circumstances? How does a newly developed belief affect specific teacher decisions and actions? Are teacher behaviors that are first influenced by new knowledge those where there is considerable time for reflection before deciding on actions (such as planning lessons), or is the initial influence on decisions that must be made quickly? Why is there considerable variance from teacher to teacher in what knowledge is assimilated and in how newly acquired knowledge affects practice?

Each of these questions can be examined with reference to either the specific pedagogical content knowledge of the type focused on in the Wisconsin Model or to pedagogical knowledge concerned with mathematics teaching practice, as previously described. Similarities and differences in how these two categories of knowledge are acquired and used by teachers is of interest.

A second component of teaching/learning paradigms that should be carefully planned is how a research project will be structured so that teachers acquire new knowledge in usable form, whether that knowledge focuses on information about learning or teaching. Teachers, like students, construct their own meaning regardless of how clearly anyone tells them things. How teachers connect this new knowledge to previous knowledge will determine not only how they use knowledge but whether they retain it. Some information can be directly told. Since teachers are thoughtful people, they will relate the new information to their previous knowledge in a way that makes sense to them. Perhaps other knowledge may be best developed through the use of group discussions, stimulated by carefully worded descriptions of particular learning situations or problems. Carefully chosen videotapes of actual classroom situations may be appropriate to use in these situations. As research accumulates, so will the opportunities to develop explanatory theories about good ways to provide information to teachers. Initially, researchers may have to use their professional judgment as to the best way to conduct knowledge-sharing sessions for teachers, and to carefully document both the training sessions and the results in classrooms.

The third and final component of teaching/learning paradigms that merits increased attention concerns contextual factors such as the culture of the classroom, the school setting, and community influences. A few brief examples of how these factors can affect teacher decision making follow.

The attitude of a class toward learning is one aspect of the culture of a classroom that may quickly change a teacher's view of what constitutes appropriate instruction and may directly influence the instruction (s)he provides. A case study of a beginning teacher reported by Cooney (1985), for example, clearly depicts how the teacher's initial philosophy and instructional approach — in this case a problem-solving approach to mathematics instruction through the use of history, recreational puzzles, and problems — were quickly altered to a more typical philosophy and textbook approach to instruction when students were not receptive to the initial methods employed. In such a case the teacher makes use of assessment, but it is not based on student content knowledge. Instead, it involves a general assessment of a reaction of the class to the instructional methods being used. If the response is negative, a teacher frequently tries a new method.

Another example of a context factor that probably influences many instructional decisions by teachers is an emphasis on improving student scores on statewide assessment tests. These instruments frequently measure narrowly defined objectives that emphasize primarily skills and factual knowledge. It should not be surprising that teachers under heavy pressure to have their students do well on such examinations allow the tests to influence many aspects of mathematics instruction, including content selection and instructional methods. Too often the methods resorted to result in students learning skills in isolation, and an opportunity to teach for transfer and flexibility of student thinking is missed (Grouws, 1988).

Teachers make many important decisions based on numerous context factors such as those previously discussed. Factors are not limited to knowledge of individual student content knowledge and they need to be part of instructional models and carefully considered as researchers attempt to understand teacher decision making.

Explanatory Models of Teacher Decision Making

How do teachers utilize knowledge, particularly knowledge they acquire as participants in research sessions designed to make them more successful in teaching mathematics in the classroom? This issue should be considered from two perspectives. First, how do teachers use various types of knowledge to make judgments during pre- and post-lesson activities? Such activities include lesson planning, materials selection, activity writing, assessment of students' written work, and other activities where teachers have some time for reflection as part of their decision making. Information about specific ways that knowledge is employed in activities like these is needed.

The second perspective involves similar investigations of activities occurring *within* a mathematics lesson where decisions must often be made quickly with far less information and fewer resources than in outside-of-class decision making. This concern addresses decision making during the interaction portion of the lesson in which the teacher interacts with the whole class, a group of students, or an individual.

The basic principle of Cognitively Guided Instruction is that instructional decisions "should be based on careful analyses of students' knowledge" (Carpenter & Fennema, 1988, p. 12). This principle provides a framework for examining both teachers' actions and how teachers make and implement instructional decisions during the interactive part of mathematics lessons. Because classrooms are complex places, it seems reasonable that teachers construct simplified models of reality that they use in making decisions and judgments (Shavelson, 1983). What types of models do teachers construct and, in particular, are they models based on continuous assessment of an individual student's content knowledge? There is some research that supports the continuous assessment hypothesis. Among a number of interesting results from an experimental study based on the CGI model (Carpenter, Fennema, Peterson, Chiang, & Loef, 1988) is the finding that CGI treatment teachers spent significantly more time listening to students than did control teachers. Qualitative data support the notion that teachers were gathering information about student knowledge and thinking. Grouws and Cramer (1989) in a study of successful junior high problem solving teachers also found that teachers regularly evaluated student problem-solving performance. The nature and methods of assessment in that study varied from teacher to teacher.

An alternate model of how teachers make decisions and implement instruction has been put forward by Putnam and Leinhardt (1986) and studied with first- and second-grade teachers (Putnam, 1987). The Curriculum Script Model is based on the idea of a script which is an ordered set of actions for teaching a particular topic and includes the skills and concepts students are expected to learn as well as the strategies and activities that will be used in teaching the ideas (Leinhardt, 1988). Putnam (1987) further explains:

> When teaching a topic, the teacher moves through
> this curriculum script, gathering information
> from student performance cues to make *minor*
> [emphasis added] adjustments in instruction. Di-
> agnosis per se is not a primary goal; it is the
> teacher's curriculum script, rather than a model
> of the student based on detailed diagnosis, that
> determines the sequence of instruction. (p. 39)

Putnam suggests that with a class of twenty to thirty students, it may be impossible for a teacher to acquire and use
detailed information about skills specific to each student.
Further, his study provided evidence that teachers *do not*
form detailed representations of correct and faulty knowledge of individual students but rather move through curriculum scripts making minor modifications based on assessments of student knowledge. This model does seem to
meet one of the criteria set forth by Clark and Peterson
(1986); namely, that a new "model of teacher interactive decision making should reflect the finding that the majority of
teachers' reported interactive decisions are preceded by factors other than judgments made about the student" (p.
277).

Other models of teacher decision making exist. Corno
(1981), for example, indicates that teachers should monitor
and observe students' facial expressions, actions, and
voices as part of decision making involving the pace and
flow of instruction. The development and refinement of accurate models of the teacher decision-making process merit
additional discussion and should be an important future
research priority.

Quality of Instruction

Assume that a teacher has made a decision that some instructional action is needed. That decision may be based on
an assessment of student content knowledge, student motivation levels, or some other factor. The decision may call
for the teacher to ask a question, give an example, draw a
diagram, or to silent. Each of these actions has a quality di-

mension associated with it. It is relatively easy to identify actions that would fall at the extreme ends of a quality continuum: making diagrams that cannot be read, asking ambiguous questions, using examples that do not fit the conditions of a definition, and so on. There is no denying, however, that making valid judgments of instructional quality require consideration of the classroom context in which the instruction is occurring. Teaching actions do have a quality dimension that includes appropriateness.

Quality considerations cannot be limited to isolated instructional behaviors; indeed, that may be the least productive way to proceed. Rather, attention should be given to the way classroom events fit together to form a meaningful learning situation. This does not mean that a lesson must be considered as a whole. Examination of components that are common to many lessons, such as review, development, seatwork, and so on, may be one manageable and productive way to proceed.

The development portion of the lesson, that part of the lesson where the focus is on facilitating the meaningful acquisition of new ideas by the learner (Good, Grouws, & Ebmeier, 1983) would be a natural starting place for this type of research. Investigations might initially examine how well various types of teacher pedagogical content knowledge (Carpenter, Fennema, Peterson, & Carey, 1988) are used; how well teachers link form to understanding (see Hiebert, 1984 for a discussion of three sites where this work might focus); or how well teachers attend to dimensions of development, such as prerequisite knowledge, generality of concepts, relationships between ideas, and so on (Good, Grouws, & Ebmeier, 1983). Regardless of the philosophical perspective of the researcher, attention to quality dimensions of instruction is needed.

Compromise in Classroom Instruction

Currently there exist some reasonably well-accepted premises about student learning. Most researchers would agree that students must be actively involved in the learning process, that they construct their own meanings, that what is learned is better retained and transferred to new situations if it is linked in meaningful ways to previous knowledge, that multiple associations between new knowledge and existing knowledge is beneficial, that practice is an important part of skill learning, and that systematic review and maintenance is necessary in order to keep knowledge and skills at high levels of recall and proficiency. If these are taken without argument, what does this imply for the teacher? Is it reasonable to expect a teacher to have an accurate picture of the existing knowledge structure of the twenty-six students in his/her class and to update it continuously? Obviously there will be considerable differences among the students in the class on just the dimension of existing knowledge, without consideration of differences in such areas as motivation levels, interest levels, and so on. Given the complexity of this situation, must teachers work with a simplified model of the reality of the classroom? Does this reduction require some compromises? That is, would teachers facilitate learning differently if there were only one student to work with instead of twenty-six? Should our models of the teacher decision-making process take better account of the realities of the classroom by considering what compromises teachers must make in working with large groups of students? Should there be a consideration of models where teachers use subsets of the class for reference purposes as was proposed some time ago by Dahllof and Lundgren (1970) with their concept of steering groups? The answers to such questions are not clear but the questions do merit attention and discussion.

SUMMARY

It is encouraging that mathematics educators are seriously reflecting on their research endeavors with an emphasis on improvement. Building on the research base that exists in both teaching and learning to develop new and better models of learning from instruction (classroom teaching) is a very promising development and we should move these ideas forward in an intellectually rigorous way. With the latter point in mind, I have suggested several issues that deserve attention. We must consider teachers to be thoughtful, reflective, professionals in all aspects of our deliberations about instruction and research. This means, for example, that teachers' decisions are influenced by a wide variety of factors both within and outside the classroom. It means that teachers are actively seeking ways to implement knowledge received in research sessions, and that it is probably unrealistic to think that we do not convey some of these ways both directly and indirectly in such sessions. In these and other ways it is important to keep the valuable premise of teachers as thoughtful decision makers in the foreground.

Second is the assumption that teachers need additional knowledge of several different varieties to make good classroom decisions. It seems academic that teachers would also benefit from being provided with information about successful teaching practices in addition to information about student knowledge in specific content domains. How teachers should acquire this knowledge base needs further study. My own bias is that these teachers as mature, thoughtful individuals can be directly presented with potentially useful information and, further, that they can be counted on to assimilate and use only that information that fits with their past experience and knowledge. Other researchers will probably not want anything presented directly, but both positions are worthy of discussion, and research employing both strategies should be conducted.

Third, more emphasis needs to be given to models of the teacher decision-making process in the classroom. I have tried to make the case for including a large variety of factors in such models and for considering models in which part of the decision-making process involves reducing the complexity of the classroom situation to a more manageable form, even though this may mean compromising the methods that would be used if a teacher were working with a single child.

Finally, the issue of quality of instruction must be an integral part of all the discussions and decisions associated with building a better understanding of successful class-room teaching of mathematics.

REFERENCES

Carpenter, T. P., & Fennema, E. (1988). *Research and cognitively guided instruction.* Madison, WI: National Center for Research in Mathematical Sciences Education.

Carpenter, T. P., Fennema, E., Peterson, P. L., & Carey, D. A. (1988). Teachers' pedagogical content knowledge of students' problem solving in elementary arithmetic. *Journal for Research in Mathematics Education, 19*(5), 385–401.

Carpenter, T. P., Fennema, E., Peterson, P. L., Chiang, C., & Loef, M. (1988, April). *Using knowledge of children's mathematical thinking in classroom teaching: An experimental study.* Paper presented at the annual meeting of the American Educational Research Association, New Orleans.

Clark, C. M., & Peterson, P. L. (1986). Teachers' thought processes. In M. C. Wittrock (Ed.), *Handbook of research on teaching* (3rd ed., pp. 255–296). New York: Macmillan.

Cobb, P., Wood, T., & Yackel, E. (in press). Learning through problem solving: A constructivist approach to second grade mathematics. In E. von Glasersfeld (Ed.), *Constructivism in mathematics education.* Dordrecht, Holland: Reidel.

Cooney, T. J. (1985). A beginning teacher's view of problem solving. *Journal for Research in Mathematics Education, 16*, 324–336.

Cooney, T. J., Grouws, D. A., & Jones, D. (1988). An agenda for research on teaching mathematics. In D. A. Grouws, T. J. Cooney, & D. Jones (Eds.), *Research agenda for mathematics education: Effective mathematics teaching* (pp. 253–261). Hillsdale, NJ: Lawrence Erlbaum Associates and Reston, VA: National Council of Teachers of Mathematics.

Corno, L. (1981). Cognitive organizing in classrooms. *Curriculum Inquiry, 11*, 359–377.

Dahllof, U., & Lundgren, U. P. (1970). *Macro- and micro-approaches combined for curriculum process analysis: A Swedish educational field project.* Göteborg, Sweden: University of Göteborg, Institute of Education.

Good, T. L., Grouws, D. A., & Ebmeier, H. (1983). *Active mathematics teaching.* New York: Longman.

Good, T. L., Grouws, D. A., & Mason, D. (1990). Teachers' beliefs about small-group instruction in elementary school mathematics. *Journal for Research in Mathematics Education, 21,* 2–15.

Grouws, D. A. (1988). One point of view: Teaching tomorrow's skills responsibly. *Arithmetic Teacher, 36*(2), 6–11.

Grouws, D. A., Cooney, T. J., and Jones, D. (Eds.) (1988). *Perspectives on research on effective mathematics teaching.* Hillsdale, NJ: Lawrence Erlbaum Associates and Reston, VA: National Council of Teachers of Mathematics.

Grouws, D. A., & Cramer, K. (1989). Teaching practices and student affect in problem solving lessons of select junior high mathematics teachers. In D. B. McLeod & V. M. Adams (Eds.), *Affect and mathematical problem solving: A new perspective* (pp. 149–161). New York: Springer-Verlag.

Hiebert, J. (1984). Children's mathematical learning: The struggle to link form and understanding. *Elementary School Journal, 84*(5), 497–513.

Leinhardt, G. (1988). Expertise in instructional lessons: An example from fractions. In D. A. Grouws, T. J. Cooney, & D. Jones (Eds.), *Research agenda for mathematics education: Effective mathematics teaching* (pp. 47–66). Hillsdale, NJ: Lawrence Erlbaum Associates and Reston, VA: National Council of Teachers of Mathematics.

Putnam, R. T. (1987). Structuring and adjusting content for students: A study of live and simulated tutoring of addition. *American Educational Research Journal, 42,* 13–48.

Putnam, R. T., & Leinhardt, G. (1986, April). *Curriculum scripts and the adjustment of content in mathematics lessons.* Paper presented at the annual meeting of the American Educational Research Association, San Francisco.

Shavelson, R. J. (1983). Review of research on teachers' pedagogical judgments, plans, and decisions. *Elementary School Journal, 83*(4), 392–413.

Shavelson, R. J., & Stern, P. (1981). Research on teachers' pedagogical thoughts, judgments, decisions, and behavior. *Review of Educational Research, 51,* 455–498.

Shulman, L. S. (1986). Those who understand: Knowledge growth in teaching. *Educational Researcher, 15*(2), 4–14.

Shulman, L. S., & Elstein, A. S. (1975). Studies of problem solving, judgment, and decision making: Implications for educational research. In F. N. Kerlinger (Ed.), *Review of research in education* (Vol. 3, pp. 3–42). Itasca, IL: F. E. Peacock.

List of Contributors

Merlyn J. Behr, Northern Illinois University
Thomas P. Carpenter, University of Wisconsin-Madison
Paul Cobb, Purdue University
Elizabeth Fennema, University of Wisconsin-Madison
Douglas A. Grouws, University of Missouri-Columbia
Guershon Harel, University of Minnesota
James Hiebert, University of Delaware
Magdalene Lampert, Michigan State University
Richard Lesh, Educational Testing Service
Douglas B. McLeod, Washington State University
Thomas R. Post, University of Minnesota
Walter G. Secada, University of Wisconsin-Madison
Diana Wearne, University of Delaware
Terry Wood, Purdue University
Erna Yackel, Purdue University-Calumet

INDEX

219